"INSPIRED *is the authority on how to build a product that customers actually want. It's not about hiring product managers - it's about establishing a culture that puts the user first, and builds the organization and teams around that customer to ensure that you are building the best product possible. From CEOs to APMs, this is required reading.*"
—Amanda Richardson, Chief Data and Strategy Officer, HotelTonight

"*We first started working with Marty when ImmobilienScout was entering growth-stage, and he helped us set the organization up to rapidly scale and grow to become one of the largest and most successful technology startups in Germany. He remained a friend and advisor to the company for many years. His book* INSPIRED *helped people from all across the company, and the new version is sure to help many more companies.*"
—Jürgen Böhm, Co-Founder, Immobilien Scout GmbH

"*It does not matter if you are a seasoned product leader or a new product manager,* INSPIRED *will make you realise that you have the best job in the world and can have incredible impact - especially if you follow Marty Cagan's words of wisdom. His book has been the bible of our industry for the past decade, and it will no doubt continue to be so with this latest update containing the most exciting best-in-class product practices.*"
—Tanya Cordrey, former Chief Digital Officer at Guardian News & Media

"*Building a great product that nails Product/Market Fit is always a key first step to any successful start-up. However, organizing the product and engineering teams, in ways that ensures scalability, speed, and quality is usually the next biggest challenge. Marty's insights and lessons learned can be applied to build highly productive teams to manage through dependencies, and build a culture that is positioned to scale. This applies whether your business is in need of a serious course correction, or on a rocket ship.*"
—Scott Sahadi, Founder and CEO, The Experience Engine

"*Marty offers actionable advice on product management without being too prescriptive, making his wisdom applicable in many contexts. He draws from a wealth of experience, illustrating his advice with dozens of real-world stories. If you want to create digital products that people love, this book will get you started on the right path.*"

—Teresa Torres, Discovery Coach

"*We have worked closely with Marty shaping product and building product management organisations in several of our portfolio companies. Marty's insight and advice is leading-edge and world-class.*"

—Harry Nellis, Partner, Accel

"*Early in my career in Product Management, I had the good fortune of meeting Marty Cagan. Since then, he has been an incredible mentor for me and the teams I've led. I have seen, firsthand at multiple companies, how Marty transforms product teams and unlocks sustained innovation and growth. Marty literally and figuratively wrote the book on Product Management for today's technology industry.*"

—Sarah Fried Rose, Product Leader and COO

"*I've been lucky to work with some of the best product managers and product minds in the business. In my experience Marty Cagan is hands down the absolute best product management mind alive today. This book packs years of experience into 250 pages.*"

—Marty Abbott, CEO, AKF Partners, former CTO, eBay

"*Great products delight customers. Marty Cagan has led and inspired countless product teams and in* INSPIRED, *you will learn how to build those products, both strategically and tactically.*"

—Shripriya Mahesh, Partner, Omidyar Network

"CEOs, Chief Product Officers, and anyone who cares about creating great products, must read this book. Your customers will love you for it."
—Phil Terry, Founder and CEO of Collaborative Gain, co-author, Customers Included

"Marty is not only a seasoned expert on all aspects of the often ambiguous discipline of product management, his book also provides inspiration, tools and techniques, and really practical help."
—Judy Gibbons, Startup Advisor and Board Member

"Building great products is hard. Marty gives great insight into best practices and skills that really can only be discovered after years of experience and study. Just about every product person I respect learned product management from INSPIRED."
—Jason Li, CEO and Founder, Boolan, Shanghai

"If you want your customers to love your products, INSPIRED is an 'everyone in the company' must read book."
—Jana Eggers, CEO, Nara Logic

"What I really love about working with Marty is that his techniques are applicable to building really great enterprise products - not just new consumer apps. INSPIRED is our true north. Anytime I feel the organization moving sideways, it's time to read it again!"
—Jeff Trom, Founder and CTO, Workiva

"I've known Marty for nearly 20 years. By now, you'd think I'd have heard everything he has to say. And yet, every time I see him, his continued interest in learning about our field means that he always new *ideas to share. And with honesty, humanity, frankness, and most of all ... perspective that never fails to give me fresh energy and a new approach. Thrilled that he's bottled it for us once more in this new edition of* INSPIRED*!"*

—Audrey Crane, Partner, DesignMap

"Marty's practical approach to building great products transformed the way we approached product development for the radical betterment of the Company and our customers. Just as importantly, his methodology helped shape multiple people's career trajectories both inside the Company and outside of it as they've gone on to drive product development in other organizations - from Fortune 500 companies to other VC backed high growth companies. If you're in a leadership role or on the product team at an organization trying to build products your target audience loves, this should be the next book you read."

—Shawn Boyer, Founder, Snagajob and goHappy

"When I needed to stand up a productive, scalable product management function at Etsy, I turned to Marty. His playbook for establishing product management as a distinct discipline is invaluable for any team working on products powered by software and made by engineers." Rarely is a business book so clearly written and packed full of concrete advice. We used it as our product management guide in scaling Etsy, and I've used it in every company since."

—Maria Thomas, Board Member and Investor

"The art of Product Management is the art of life itself. Surround your-selves by great people, focus on your mojo, build great stuff with integrity, hold strong opinions but lightly. And Marty is one of the best teachers of this art."

—Punit Soni, Founder and CEO, Robin, Former Google APM

"*Marty was a coach and mentor for my early years in product management and the book* INSPIRED *became the go to guide whenever I needed some clarity on the product manager's role, skill set or the daily challenges from product discovery to execution. And it still was a solid reference while stepping up to a product leadership role. Now, in my role as discovery coach, I recommend the book to every new client. It's not a methodology book; this book helps product people to get the right mindset regardless of the frameworks and techniques they are using.*"

—Petra Wille, Discovery Coach

"*Marty's 2nd Edition builds on an amazing base of knowledge and experience, and provides even more insights, lessons, and frameworks that are imperative to every product-based company.*"

—Chuck Geiger, CTO/CPO Chegg

"*Marty has a way of elegantly simplifying decades of experience leading and teaching product organizations to excel in value creation for their customers into one actionable, inspiring, quick read. From organizational assessments, tools for aligning teams against a real user need, to the nitty gritty of pulling off continuous product discovery & delivery,* INSPIRED *is my go-to reference and recommendation for any Product Leader looking to up their game for the sake of building winning products.*"

—Lisa Kavanaugh, Executive Coach

"*Marty is legendary among the best product leaders for cutting to the heart of where their teams need to improve. His advice is practical, actionable and will excite you and your team to better address customer needs immediately. Your engineers and customers will thank you for reading this book.*"

—Hope Gurion, Product Leader

INSPIRED

INSPIRED

HOW TO
CREATE
TECH
PRODUCTS
CUSTOMERS
LOVE

SECOND EDITION

MARTY CAGAN
Founder, Silicon Valley Product Group

Published by John Wiley & Sons, Inc., Hoboken, New Jersey.

Published simultaneously in Canada.

For general information about our other products and services, please contact our Customer Care Department within the United States at (800) 762-2974, outside the United States at (317) 572-3993 or fax (317) 572-4002.

Wiley publishes in a variety of print and electronic formats and by print-on-demand. Some material included with standard print versions of this book may not be included in e-books or in print-on-demand. If this book refers to media such as a CD or DVD that is not included in the version you purchased, you may download this material at http://booksupport.wiley.com. For more information about Wiley products, visit www.wiley.com.

Library of Congress Cataloging-in-Publication Data is Available:

ISBN 9781119387503 (Hardcover)
ISBN 9781119387541 (ePDF)
ISBN 9781119387565 (ePub)

Cover Design: Wiley
Cover Image: © John Lawson/Getty Images

Printed in the United States of America

SKY10022093_110220

This book is dedicated to my father, Carl Cagan. In 1969, he received the first PhD in computer science in the United States (prior to that computer science was part of electrical engineering programs), and he authored the first book on databases (Data Management Systems, in 1973, also by John Wiley & Sons).

In addition to being a terrific father, he taught me to program a computer when I was nine years old—decades before this became a thing—and he instilled in me a love of technology when so many of the technologies we depend on today were just being conceived.

CONTENTS

Preface to the Second Edition   *xvii*

**PART I   LESSONS FROM TOP TECH
            COMPANIES**   1

   Chapter 1   Behind Every Great Product   5

   Chapter 2   Technology-Powered Products
   and Services   7

   Chapter 3   Startups: Getting to Product/Market Fit   9

   Chapter 4   Growth-Stage Companies: Scaling
   to Success   11

   Chapter 5   Enterprise Companies: Consistent
   Product Innovation   13

   Chapter 6   The Root Causes of Failed Product
   Efforts   15

   Chapter 7   Beyond Lean and Agile   23

   Chapter 8   Key Concepts   25

PART II   THE RIGHT PEOPLE   31

  PRODUCT TEAMS   32

   Chapter 9   Principles of Strong Product Teams   33

   Chapter 10 The Product Manager   41

Chapter 11   The Product Designer   53

Chapter 12   The Engineers   59

Chapter 13   Product Marketing Managers   63

Chapter 14   The Supporting Roles   67

Chapter 15   Profile: Jane Manning of Google   71

PEOPLE @ SCALE   74

Chapter 16   The Role of Leadership   75

Chapter 17   The Head of Product Role   79

Chapter 18   The Head of Technology Role   87

Chapter 19   The Delivery Manager Role   91

Chapter 20   Principles of Structuring Product Teams   93

Chapter 21   Profile: Lea Hickman of Adobe   103

PART III   THE RIGHT PRODUCT   107

PRODUCT ROADMAPS   108

Chapter 22   The Problems with Product Roadmaps   111

Chapter 23   The Alternative to Roadmaps   115

PRODUCT VISION   121

Chapter 24   Product Vision and Product Strategy   123

Chapter 25   Principles of Product Vision   129

Chapter 26   Principles of Product Strategy   133

Chapter 27   Product Principles   135

PRODUCT OBJECTIVES   137

Chapter 28   The OKR Technique   139

Chapter 29   Product Team Objectives   143

PRODUCT @ SCALE   146

Chapter 30   Product Objectives @ Scale   147

Chapter 31   Product Evangelism   151

Chapter 32   Profile: Alex Pressland of the BBC   155

PART IV   THE RIGHT PROCESS   159

PRODUCT DISCOVERY   161

Chapter 33   Principles of Product Discovery   165

Chapter 34   Discovery Techniques Overview   171

DISCOVERY FRAMING TECHNIQUES   175

Chapter 35   Opportunity Assessment Technique   179

Chapter 36   Customer Letter Technique   183

Chapter 37   Startup Canvas Technique   187

DISCOVERY PLANNING TECHNIQUES   191

Chapter 38   Story Map Technique   193

Chapter 39   Customer Discovery Program
                 Technique   195

Chapter 40   Profile: Martina Lauchengco
                 of Microsoft   205

DISCOVERY IDEATION TECHNIQUES   208

Chapter 41   Customer Interviews   211

Chapter 42   Concierge Test Technique   215

Chapter 43   The Power of Customer Misbehavior   217

Chapter 44   Hack Days   221

DISCOVERY PROTOTYPING TECHNIQUES   223

Chapter 45   Principles of Prototypes   227

Chapter 46   Feasibility Prototype Technique   229

Chapter 47   User Prototype Technique   233

Chapter 48   Live-Data Prototype Technique   235

Chapter 49   Hybrid Prototype Technique   239

DISCOVERY TESTING TECHNIQUES   241

Chapter 50   Testing Usability   243

Chapter 51   Testing Value   251

Chapter 52   Demand Testing Techniques   253

Chapter 53 Qualitative Value Testing Techniques 259

Chapter 54 Quantitative Value Testing Techniques 265

Chapter 55 Testing Feasibility 273

Chapter 56 Testing Business Viability 277

Chapter 57 Profile: Kate Arnold of Netflix 283

TRANSFORMATION TECHNIQUES 286

Chapter 58 Discovery Sprint Technique 287

Chapter 59 Pilot Team Technique 291

Chapter 60 Weaning an Organization Off Roadmaps 293

PROCESS @ SCALE 295

Chapter 61 Managing Stakeholders 297

Chapter 62 Communicating Product Learnings 305

Chapter 63 Profile: Camille Hearst of Apple 307

PART V THE RIGHT CULTURE 309

Chapter 64 Good Product Team/Bad Product Team 311

Chapter 65 Top Reasons for Loss of Innovation 315

Chapter 66 Top Reasons for Loss of Velocity 319

Chapter 67 Establishing a Strong Product Culture 323

Acknowledgments 327
About the Author 329
Learning More 331
Index 333

Preface to the Second Edition

When I first considered publishing an update to the first edition of my book *INSPIRED*, I estimated that maybe I would modify something like 10–20 percent of the content. That's because there was very little of the first edition that I wished I could change.

However, once I got started, I quickly realized that this second edition would require a complete rewrite. Not because I regretted what I had written, but because I believe I have much better ways of explaining these topics now.

I had no idea that the first edition would be as successful as it has been. Thanks to the book, I have made friends all over the globe. The book has been translated into several languages, and despite being nearly 10 years old as of this writing, sales continues to grow, all by word of mouth and reviews.

So, if you have read the first edition, I thank you, and hope you enjoy the second edition even more. If you are new to *INSPIRED*, I am hoping this new edition accomplishes its objective even better.

When I wrote the first edition, it was before Agile was well established in product companies, and before Customer Development and Lean Startup nomenclature became popularized. Today, most teams have been using these techniques for several years and are more interested in what's beyond Lean and Agile, which is what I focus on here.

I have kept the basic structure of the book intact, but the techniques I describe have improved significantly over the past decade.

Beyond changing how I explain the topics and updating the techniques, the other major change to the book is that I now go into detail on what I refer to here as Product @ Scale.

In the first edition, I focused more on startups. In this edition, however, I wanted to expand the scope to look at the challenges of growth-stage companies and how product can be done well at large, enterprise companies.

There's no question that scale introduces serious challenges, and over the past decade, much of my time has been spent coaching companies through rapid growth. Sometimes we call that surviving success, if that gives you an indication of how hard it can be.

I've received a lot of great feedback from readers of the first edition, and there are a couple of important things I've learned that I would like to address here.

First, there really is a critical need to focus on the specific job of the product manager. In the first edition, I talked a lot about product management, but I tried to speak to product teams more broadly. Today, there are many excellent resources for product designers and engineers, but precious little available specifically for *product managers* who are responsible for *technology-powered* products. So, in this edition I decided to concentrate on the job of the technology product manager. If you are a product manager at a technology company, or if you aspire to be one, I am hoping this will become your go-to resource.

Second, there are many people looking for a recipe for product success—a prescriptive guide or framework to how to create products customers love. While I understand the desire, and I know I'd likely sell many more copies if I positioned this book that way, the unfortunate truth is that's just not how great products are created. It is much more about creating the right product culture for success, and understanding the array of product discovery and delivery techniques so that you can use the right tool for the specific issue you are facing. And, yes, this means that the job of the product manager is not in any sense easy, and truth be told, not everyone is equipped to succeed in this job.

All that said, the tech product management job is today one of the most desired jobs in our industry, and is the leading source—the proving ground—of startup CEOs. So, if you've got the desire and are willing to put in the effort, I'd like nothing better than to help you succeed.

I

Lessons from Top Tech Companies

In the mid-1980s, I was a young software engineer working for Hewlett Packard on a high-profile product. It was a time (the first time) when artificial intelligence was all the rage, and I was fortunate enough to be working at what was then one of the industry's best technology companies, as part of a very strong software engineering team (several members of that team went on to substantial success in companies across the industry).

Our assignment was a difficult one: to deliver AI-enabling technology on a low-cost, general-purpose workstation that, until then, required a special-purpose hardware/software combination that cost more than $100,000 per user—a price few could afford.

We worked long and hard for well over a year, sacrificing countless nights and weekends. Along the way, we added several patents to HP's portfolio. We developed the software to meet HP's exacting quality standards. We internationalized the product and localized it for several languages. We trained the sales force. We previewed our technology with the press and received excellent reviews. We were ready. We released. We celebrated the release.

Just one problem: No one bought it.

The product was a complete failure in the marketplace. Yes, it was technically impressive, and the reviewers loved it, but it wasn't something people wanted or needed.

The team was of course extremely frustrated with this outcome. But soon we began to ask ourselves some very important questions: Who decides what products we should build? How do they decide? How do they know that what we build will be useful?

Our young team learned something very profound—something many teams have discovered the hard way: *It doesn't matter how good your engineering team is if they are not given something worthwhile to build.*

When trying to track down the root cause of our failure, I learned that the decisions about what to build came from a product manager—someone who generally resided in the marketing organization and who was responsible for defining the products we built. But I also learned that product management wasn't something HP was particularly good at. I later learned that most companies weren't good at this either, and, in fact, most still aren't.

I promised myself that never again would I work so hard on a product unless I knew the product would be something that users and customers wanted.

Over the next 30 years, I have had the very good fortune to work on some of the most successful high-tech products of our time—first at HP during the rise of personal computers; then at Netscape Communications during the rise of the Internet, where I worked as vice president of platform and tools; later at eBay during the rise of e-commerce and marketplaces, where I served as the senior vice president of product and design; and then as an adviser to startups working with many of what have become today's most successful technology product companies.

Not every product effort has been as successful as others, but I am happy to say that none were failures, and several became loved and used by millions of people around the world.

Soon after I left eBay, I started getting calls from product organizations wanting to improve how they produced products. As I began working with these companies, I discovered that there was a tremendous difference between how the *best* companies produced products and how *most* companies produced them.

> *I discovered that there was a tremendous difference between how the best companies produced products and how most companies produced them.*

I realized that *the state of the art was very different from the state of the practice*.

Most companies were still using old and inefficient ways to discover and deliver products. I also learned that there was precious little help available, either from academia, including the best business school programs, or from industry organizations, which seemed hopelessly stuck in the failed models of the past—just like the one I worked in at HP.

I have had some great rides, and I am especially thankful that I have had the chance to work for and with some of the best product minds in the industry. The best ideas in this book are from these people. You will find a list of many of them in the acknowledgments. I have learned from them all, and I am grateful to each one of them.

I chose this career because I wanted to work on products that customers love—products that inspire and provide real value. I find that most product leaders also want to create inspiring and successful products. But most products are not inspiring, and life is too short for bad products.

My hope in writing this book is that it will help share the best practices of the most successful product companies and that the result will be truly inspiring products—products that customers love.

1

Behind Every Great Product

I t is my strong belief, and the central concept driving this book, that behind every great product there is someone—usually someone behind the scenes, working tirelessly—who led the product team to combine technology and design to solve real customer problems in a way that met the needs of the business.

These people usually have the title *product manager*, but they might be a startup co-founder or CEO, or they might be someone in another role on the team who stepped up because they saw the need.

Further, this product management role is very distinct from the design, engineering, marketing, or project manager roles.

This book is intended for these people.

Within modern technology product teams, the product manager has some very specific and very challenging responsibilities. It's a tremendously difficult job, and anyone who tries to tell you otherwise is not doing you any favors.

The product manager role is usually very much a full-time assignment. I don't personally know many who are able to do what they need to do in less than 60 hours a week.

It's great if you're a designer or an engineer who also wants to serve as a product manager—there are some real advantages to that. But you'll find out pretty quickly that you're taking on an immense amount of work. If you're up for that, however, the results can be impressive.

> *It is my strong belief, and the central concept driving this book, that behind every great product there is someone—usually someone behind the scenes, working tirelessly—who led the product team to combine technology and design to solve real customer problems in a way that met the needs of the business.*

A product team is comprised of at least a product manager and usually somewhere between 2 and 10 engineers. If you're creating a user-facing product, you would expect to have a product designer on your team as well.

In this book, we explore the situation wherein you might have to use engineers or designers in a different location or from an agency or outsourcing firm. But regardless of how you assemble your team, this job and this book assume you have a team assigned to work with you to design, to build, and to deliver a product.

2

Technology-Powered Products and Services

There are many kinds of products out there, but in this book, I concentrate exclusively on products that are *powered by technology*.

Some of what we explore in this book may help you if you're building non-tech products, but there are no guarantees in that case. Frankly, there are already a wide variety of readily accessible resources for non-tech products such as most consumer packaged goods, and for product managers of these non-tech products.

My focus is on the unique issues and challenges associated with building technology-powered products, services, and experiences.

Some good examples of the sweet spot that we explore are consumer-service products, such as e-commerce sites or marketplaces (e.g., Netflix, Airbnb, or Etsy), social media (e.g., Facebook, LinkedIn, or Twitter), business services (e.g., Salesforce.com, Workday, or Workiva), consumer devices (e.g., Apple, Sonos, or Tesla), and mobile applications (e.g., Uber, Audible, or Instagram).

Technology-powered prod-
ucts do not need to be purely
digital. Many of the best examples
today are blends of online and
offline experiences—like finding a
ride or a room for the night, getting a home loan, or sending an
overnight package.

> *My focus is on the unique
> issues and challenges
> associated with building
> technology-powered
> products, services, and
> experiences.*

It's my belief that most products today are transforming into
technology-powered products, and the companies that don't realize this
are rapidly being disrupted. But, again, I'm only focused here on
technology-powered products, and those companies that believe they
must embrace technology and consistently innovate on behalf of their
customers.

3

Startups: Getting to Product/Market Fit

In the technology world, we generally have three stages of companies: startups, growth-stage, and enterprise companies. Let's briefly consider how we characterize each one of these stages, and the challenges you are likely to face in each.

I loosely define *startup* as a new product company that has yet to achieve product/market fit. Product/market fit is an extremely important concept that I'll define in the pages that follow, but for now, let's just say that the startup is still trying to come up with a product that can power a viable business.

In a startup, the product manager role is usually covered by one of the co-founders. Typically, there are fewer than 25 engineers, covering a range of from one product team up to maybe four or five.

The reality of startup life is that you're in a race to achieve product/market fit before you run out of money. Nothing else much matters until you can come up with a strong product that meets the needs of an initial market, so most of the focus of the young company is necessarily on the product.

Startups usually have a limited amount of early funding, intended to determine if the company can discover and deliver the necessary product. The closer you come to running out of money, the more frantic the pace and the more desperate the team and the leadership becomes.

While money and time are typically tight, good startups are optimized to learn and move quickly, and there's normally very little bureaucracy to slow them down. Yet the very high failure rate of technology startups is no secret. The few that succeed are usually those that are really good at product discovery, which is a major topic of this book.

Working at a startup—racing toward product/market fit—is usually stressful, exhausting, and risky. But it can also be an amazingly positive experience, and if things go well, a financially rewarding one too.

> *Nothing else much matters until you can come up with a strong product that meets the needs of an initial market.*

4

Growth-Stage Companies: Scaling to Success

Those startups skilled and fortunate enough (it usually takes both) to get to product/market fit are ready to tackle another equally difficult challenge: how to effectively grow and scale.

There are many very significant challenges involved in growing and scaling a startup into a large, successful business. While it's an extremely difficult challenge, it is, as we say, a good problem to have.

In addition to hiring lots more people, we need to figure out how to replicate our earlier successes with new, adjacent products and services. At the same time, we need to grow the core business as fast as possible.

In growth stage, we typically have somewhere between about 25 and several hundred engineers, so there are many more people around to help, but the signs of organizational stress are everywhere.

Product teams complain that they don't understand the big picture—they don't see how their work contributes to the larger goals, and they're struggling with what it means to be an empowered, autonomous team.

While it's an extremely difficult challenge, it is, as we say, a good problem to have.

Sales and marketing often complain that the go-to-market strategies that worked for the first product are not so appropriate for some of the new products in the portfolio.

The technology infrastructure that was created to meet the needs of the initial product is often bursting at the seams, and you start to hear the term "technical debt" from every engineer you speak with.

This stage is also tough on leaders because the leadership style and mechanisms that worked while the company was a young startup often fail to scale. Leaders are forced to change their roles and, in many cases, their behaviors.

But the motivation to overcome these challenges is very strong. The company is often in pursuit of a public offering or, perhaps, becoming a major business unit of an existing company. As well as the very real possibility of having a significant and positive impact on the world can be very motivating.

5

Enterprise Companies: Consistent Product Innovation

For those companies that succeed in scaling and that want to create a lasting business, some of the toughest challenges still lie ahead.

Strong tech-product companies know they need to ensure consistent product innovation. This means constantly creating new value for their customers and for their business. Not just tweaking and optimizing existing products (referred to as value capture) but, rather, developing each product to reach its full potential.

Yet, many large, enterprise companies have already embarked on a slow death spiral. They become all about leveraging the value and the brand that was created many years or even decades earlier. The death of an enterprise company rarely happens overnight, and a large company can stay afloat for many years. But, make no mistake about it, the organization is sinking, and the end state is all but certain.

It's not intentional, of course, but once companies reach this size—often becoming a publicly traded company—there are a tremendous number of stakeholders throughout the business

> *Strong tech-product companies know they need to ensure consistent product innovation.*

working hard to protect what the company has created. Unfortunately, this often means shutting down new initiatives or ventures that could re-create the business (but potentially put the core business at risk), or putting up so many obstacles to new ideas that few people are willing or able to drive the company in a new direction.

The symptoms of this are hard to miss, starting with diminished morale, the lack of innovation, and how much slower it is for new product work to get into the hands of customers.

When the company was young, it likely had a clear and compelling vision. When it achieves enterprise stage, however, the company has largely achieved that original vision and now people aren't sure what's next. Product teams complain about the lack of vision, lack of empowerment, the fact that it takes forever to get a decision made, and product work is turning into design by committee.

Leadership is likely frustrated, too, with the lack of innovation from the product teams. All too often, they resort to acquisitions or creating separate "innovation centers" to incubate new businesses in a protected environment. Yet this rarely results in the innovation they're so desperate for.

And you'll also hear lots of talk about how it is that large, enterprise companies such as Adobe, Amazon, Apple, Facebook, Google, and Netflix have been able to avoid this fate. The organization's leadership team wonders why they can't do the same. The fact is they *could* do the same. But they'll need to make some pretty big changes, and that's what this book is about.

6

The Root Causes of Failed Product Efforts

Let's start by exploring the root causes of why so many product efforts fail.

I see the same basic way of working at the vast majority of companies, of every size, in every corner of the globe, and I can't help but notice that this is not close to how the best companies actually work.

Let me warn you that this discussion can be a little depressing, especially if it hits too close to home, so if that's the case, I'll ask you to hang in there with me.

Figure 6.1 describes the process that most companies still use to create products. I'll try not to editorialize yet—let me first just describe the process:

As you can see, everything starts with *ideas*. In most companies, they're coming from inside (executives or key stakeholders or business owners) or outside (current or prospective customers). Wherever the ideas originate, there are always a whole bunch of things that different parts of the business need us to do.

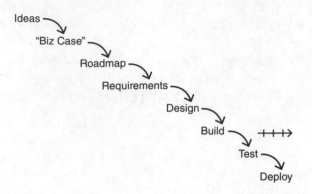

FIGURE 6.1 Root Causes of Failed Product Efforts

Now, most companies want to prioritize those ideas into a *roadmap*, and they do this for two main reasons. First, they want us to work on the most important things first, and second, they want to be able to predict when things will be ready.

To accomplish this, there is usually some form of *quarterly or annual planning session* in which the leaders consider the ideas and negotiate a product roadmap. But in order to prioritize, they first need some form of a *business case* for each item.

Some companies do formal business cases, and some are informal, but either way it boils down to the need to know two things about each idea: (1) How much money or value will it make? and (2) How much money or time will it cost? This information is then used to come up with the roadmap, usually for the next quarter, but sometimes as much as a year out.

At this point, the product and technology organization has its marching orders, and they typically work the items from the highest priority on down.

Once an idea makes it to the top of the list, the first thing that's done is for a product manager to talk to the stakeholders to flesh out the idea and to come up with a set of "requirements."

These requirements might be user stories, or they might be more like some form of a functional specification. Their purpose is to communicate with the designers and engineers what needs to be built.

Once the requirements are gathered up, the *user experience design* team (assuming the company has such a team), is asked to provide the interaction design, the visual design, and, in cases of physical devices, the industrial design.

Finally, the requirements and design specs make it to *engineers*. This is usually where Agile finally enters the picture.

Anyway, the engineers will typically break up the work into a set of *iterations*—called "sprints" in the Scrum process. So maybe it takes one to three sprints to build out the idea.

Hopefully the *QA testing* is part of those sprints, but if not, the QA team will follow this up with some testing to make sure the new idea works as advertised and doesn't introduce other problems (known as *regressions*).

Once we get the green light from QA, the new idea is finally *deployed* to actual customers.

In the majority of companies that I first meet, large and small, this is essentially how they work, and have worked, for many years. Yet these same companies consistently complain about the *lack of innovation* and the *very long time* it takes to make it from idea to customers' hands.

You might recognize that while I mentioned Agile, and while almost everyone today claims to be Agile, what I've just described is very much a *waterfall* process. In fairness to the engineers, they're typically doing about as much Agile as they can, given the broader waterfall context.

Okay, so that may be what most teams do, but why is that necessarily the reason for so many problems? Let's connect the dots now, so we can clearly see why this very common way of working is responsible for most failed product efforts.

In the list that follows, I'm going to share what I consider to be the top-10 biggest problems with this way of working. Keep in mind that all 10 of these problems are *very serious issues*, any one of which could derail a team. But many companies have more than one or even all of these problems.

1. Let's start at the top—the *source of ideas*. This model leads to sales-driven specials and stakeholder-driven products. Lots more to come on this key topic, but for now, let me just say that this is

> *While almost everyone today claims to be Agile, what I've just described is very much a* waterfall *process.*

not the source of our best product ideas. Another consequence of this approach is the lack of team empowerment. In this model, they're just there to implement—they're mercenaries.

2. Next, let's talk about the fatal flaw in these *business cases*. To be clear, I'm personally in favor of doing business cases, at least for ideas that need a larger investment. But the way most companies do them at this stage to come up with a prioritized roadmap is truly ridiculous and here's why. Remember those two key inputs to every business case? How much money you'll make, and how much it will cost? Well, the cold, hard truth is that, at this stage, we have no clue about either of these. In fact, we *can't* know.

   We can't know how much money we'll make because that depends entirely on how good the solution turns out to be. If the team does an excellent job, this could be wildly successful and literally change the course of the company. The truth, however, is that many product ideas end up making absolutely nothing. And that's not an exaggeration for effect. Literally *nothing* (we know this from A/B testing).

   In any case, one of the most critical lessons in product is *knowing what we can't know*, and we just can't know at this stage how much money we'll make.

   Likewise, we have no idea what it will cost to build. Without knowing the actual solution, this is extremely hard for engineering to predict. Most experienced engineers will refuse to even give an estimate at this stage, but some are pressured into the old t-shirt sizing compromise—just let us know if this is "small, medium, large, or extra large."

   But companies really want those prioritized roadmaps, and to get one, they need some kind of system to rate the ideas. So people play the business case game.

3. An even bigger issue is what comes next, which is when companies get really excited about their *product roadmaps*. I've seen countless roadmaps over the years, and the vast majority of them are essentially prioritized lists of features and projects. Marketing needs this feature for a campaign. Sales needs this feature for a new customer. Someone wants a PayPal integration. You get the idea.

But here's the prob-
lem—maybe the biggest
problem of all. It's what I call
the *two inconvenient truths
about product*.

> *The first truth is that at
> least half of our ideas are
> just not going to work.*

The first truth is that at least *half of our ideas are just not
going to work*. There are many reasons for an idea to not work
out. The most common is that customers just aren't as excited
about this idea as we are. So, they choose not to use it. Sometimes they want to use it and they try it out, but the product is
so complicated that it's simply more trouble than it's worth, so
users again choose not to use it. Sometimes the issue is that customers would love it, but it turns out to be much more involved
to build than we thought, and we decide we simply can't afford
the time and money required to deliver it.

So, I promise you that at least half the ideas on your
roadmap are not going to deliver what you hope. (By the way,
the really good teams assume that at least three quarters of the
ideas won't perform like they hope.)

If that's not bad enough, the second inconvenient truth is
that even with the ideas that do prove to have potential, it typically takes *several iterations* to get the implementation of this
idea to the point where it delivers the necessary business value.
We call that *time to money*.

One of the most important things about product that I've
learned is that there is simply no escaping these inconvenient
truths, no matter how smart you might be. And I've had the
good fortune to work with many truly exceptional product
teams. The real difference is how you deal with these truths.

4. Next, let's consider the *role of product management* in this model.
In fact, we wouldn't call this role product management—it's
really a form of project management. In this model, it's more
about *gathering requirements and documenting them* for engineers.
At this point, let me just say that this is 180 degrees away from
the reality of modern tech product management.

5. It's a similar story with the *role of design*. It's way too late in the
game to get the real value of design, and mostly what's being

done is what we call the "lipstick on the pig" model. The damage has already been done, and now we're just trying to put a coat of paint on the mess. The UX designers know this is not good, but they try to make it look as nice and consistent as they can.

6. Maybe the biggest missed opportunity in this model is the fact that *engineering gets brought in way too late*. We say if you're just using your engineers to code, you're only getting about half their value. The little secret in product is that *engineers are typically the best single source of innovation*; yet, they are not even invited to the party in this process.

7. Not only is engineering brought in way too late, but the principles and key benefits of Agile enter the picture far too late. Teams using Agile in this way are getting maybe 20 percent of the actual value and potential of Agile methods. What you're really seeing is Agile for delivery, but the rest of the organization and context is anything but Agile.

8. This entire process is very *project-centric*. The company usually funds projects, staffs projects, pushes projects through the organization, and finally launches projects. Unfortunately, *projects are output and product is all about outcome*. This process predictably leads to orphaned projects. Yes, something was finally released, but it doesn't meet its objectives so what really was the point? In any case, it's a serious problem, and not close to how we need to build products.

9. The biggest flaw of the old waterfall process has always been, and remains, that all the risk is at the end, which means that *customer validation happens way too late*.

   The key principle in Lean methods is to reduce waste, and one of the biggest forms of waste is to design, build, test, and deploy a feature or product only to find out it is not what was needed. The irony is that many teams *believe* they're applying Lean principles; yet, they follow this basic process I've just described. And then I point out to them that they are trying out ideas in one of the most expensive, slowest ways we know.

10. Finally, while we're busy doing this process and wasting our time and money, the biggest loss of all usually turns out to be the *opportunity cost* of what the organization could have and should have been doing instead. We can't get that time or money back.

It's no surprise that so many companies spend so much time and money and get so little in return. I warned you this could be depressing. But it's critical that you have a deep understanding of exactly why your company needs to change how it works, if, indeed, your company is working this way.

The good news is I promise you that the best teams operate nothing like what I've just described.

> *It's no surprise that so many companies spend so much time and money and get so little in return.*

7

Beyond Lean and Agile

People are always searching for a silver bullet to create products, and there is always a willing industry—ready and waiting to serve with books, coaching, training, and consulting. But there is no silver bullet, and inevitably people figure this out. That's when the backlash begins. As I write this, it's in vogue to criticize both Lean and Agile.

I have no doubt that many people and teams are in some measure disappointed with the results from their adoption of both Lean and Agile. And I understand the reasons for this. That said, I am convinced that Lean and Agile values and principles are here to stay. Not so much the particular *manifestations* of these methods that many teams use today, but the core principles behind them. I would argue that they both represent meaningful progress, and I would never want to go backward on those two fronts.

But as I said, they are not silver bullets either, and as with any tool, you have to be smart about how you use it. I meet countless teams that claim to be following Lean principles; yet, they work for months on what they call an MVP, and they really don't know what they have and whether it will sell until they've spent substantial time and money—hardly in the spirit of Lean. Or they go way overboard and think they have to test and validate everything, so they go nowhere fast.

And, as I just pointed out, the way Agile is practiced in most product companies is hardly Agile in any meaningful sense.

The best product teams I know have already moved past how most teams practice these methods—leveraging the core principles of Lean and Agile, but raising the bar on what they're trying to achieve and how they work.

When I see these teams, they may frame the issues a little differently, sometimes using different nomenclature, but at the heart, I see three overarching principles at work:

1. **Risks are tackled *up front*, rather than at the end.** In modern teams, we tackle these risks *prior* to deciding to build anything. These risks include *value* risk (whether customers will buy it), *usability* risk (whether users can figure out how to use it), *feasibility* risk (whether our engineers can build what we need with the time, skills, and technology we have), and *business viability* risk (whether this solution also works for the various aspects of our business—sales, marketing, finance, legal, etc.).

2. **Products are defined and designed *collaboratively*, rather than sequentially.** They have finally moved beyond the old model in which a product manager defines requirements, a designer designs a solution that delivers on those requirements, and then engineering implements those requirements, with each person living with the constraints and decisions of the ones that preceded. In strong teams, product, design, and engineering work side by side, in a give-and-take way, to come up with technology-powered solutions that our customers love and that work for our business.

3. **Finally, it's all about *solving problems*, not implementing features.** Conventional product roadmaps are all about output. Strong teams know it's not only about implementing a solution. They must ensure that solution solves the underlying problem. It's about *business results*.

You will see that I keep these three overarching principles front and center throughout this book.

8

Key Concepts

In this book, I refer to a set of concepts that form the foundation of modern product work. I'd like to briefly explain them here.

Holistic Product

I have already been using the term *product* pretty loosely. I did say I'm only talking about technology-powered products. But, more generally, when I refer to product I mean a very holistic definition of product.

This certainly includes the *functionality*—the features.

But it also includes the *technology* that enables this functionality.

It also includes the *user experience design* that presents this functionality.

And it includes how we *monetize* this functionality.

It includes how we attract and *acquire users and customers*.

And it can also include *offline experiences* as well that are essential to delivering the product's value.

If, for example, your product is an e-commerce site, then this would include the merchandise-fulfillment experience and the merchandise-return experience. In general, for e-commerce businesses, product includes everything *except* the actual merchandise being sold.

Similarly, for a media company, we refer to the product as everything except the content.

The point is to have a very inclusive and holistic definition of *product*. You are not just concerned with implementing features.

Continuous Discovery and Delivery

I explained previously that most companies still have a process that is essentially waterfall at its core, and I told you that what we do in a modern team is very different.

We'll be going more into the product development process later, but I do need to introduce a high-level concept about process at this point in our discussion. That is, there are two essential high-level activities in all product teams. *We need to discover the product to be built, and we need to deliver that product to market.*

Discovery and delivery are our two main activities on a cross-functional product team, and they are both typically ongoing and in parallel.

There are several ways to think about this and to visualize it, but the concept is fairly simple: We are always working in parallel to both *discover* the necessary product to be built—which is primarily what the product manager and designer work on every day—while the engineers work to *deliver* production-quality product.

Now, as you'll soon see, it's a little more involved than that. For example, the engineers are also helping daily on discovery (and many of the best innovations come from that participation, so this is not a minor point), and the product manager and designer are also helping daily on delivery (mainly to clarify intended behavior). But this is what's going on at a high level.

> *We need to discover the product to be built, and we need to deliver that product to market.*

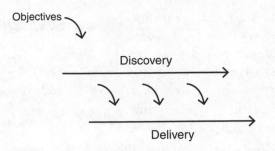

FIGURE 8.1 Continuous Discovery and Delivery

Product Discovery

Discovery is very much about the intense collaboration of product management, user experience design, and engineering. In discovery, we are tackling the various risks before we write even one line of production software.

The purpose of product discovery is to quickly separate the good ideas from the bad. The output of product discovery is a *validated product backlog*.

Specifically, this means getting answers to four critical questions:

1. Will the user buy this (or choose to use it)?
2. Can the user figure out how to use this?
3. Can our engineers build this?
4. Can our stakeholders support this?

Prototypes

Product discovery involves running a series of very quick experiments, and to do these experiments quickly and inexpensively, we use *prototypes* rather than products. At this point, let me just say that there are several types of prototypes, each for different risks and situations, but they all require *at least* an order of magnitude of less time and effort than building a product.

To set your expectations, strong teams normally test many product ideas each week—on the order of 10 to 20 or more per week.

> *To set your expectations, strong teams normally test many product ideas each week—on the order of 10 to 20 or more per week.*

I want to emphasize that these are experiments, typically run using prototypes. A prototype is not something that's ready for prime time and certainly not something your company would try to sell and stand behind. But they're immensely useful, as they're all about learning fast and cheap.

Product Delivery

The purpose of all these prototypes and experiments in discovery is to quickly come up with something that provides some evidence it is worth building and that we can then deliver to our customers.

This means the necessary scale, performance, reliability, fault tolerance, security, privacy, internationalization, and localization have been performed, and the product works as advertised.

The purpose of product delivery is to build and deliver these production-quality technology *products*, something you can sell and run a business on.

Products and Product/Market Fit

Just because we've invested the time and effort to create a robust product does not mean anyone will want to buy it. So, in the product world, we strive to achieve *product/market fit*.

This is the smallest possible actual *product* that meets the needs of a specific *market* of customers. Marc Andreessen is credited with popularizing this all-important concept, and it is a major focus of this book.

And just to be clear, since these are actual products, they are the result of *delivery*. The discovery activities help us determine the necessary product, but it is delivery that actually does the work necessary to build, test, and release the product.

Product Vision

The final critical concept is *product vision*. This refers to the longer-term objective of this product, normally 2–10 years out. It is how we as a product organization intend to deliver on the company's mission.

So, we use *prototypes* to conduct rapid experiments in product discovery, and then in delivery, we build and release *products* in hopes of achieving *product/market fit*, which is a key step on the way to delivering on the company's *product vision*.

Now don't worry if you're hazy on any of these concepts. I know you likely have many questions, but they'll hopefully become clear as we dive deeper into each topic. It's also normal to be a little skeptical—"How can I possibly run 15 of these experiments in a week?"

I warned you that strong product teams work nothing like most teams, and this should give you your first taste of how different things can be.

Minimum Viable Product

The concept of *minimum viable product* (MVP) is one of the most important concepts in the product world. It has been around for many years. The term was coined by Frank Robinson (in 2001), and I wrote about the concept in the first edition of this book (in 2008). It was popularized, however, in the book *The Lean Startup* by Eric Ries in 2011.

Eric's book did a great deal to help product teams, and to me, it is a must-read book for all product people. But I think most people would likely admit that the concept of MVP has caused considerable confusion within product teams, and I spend a lot of my time helping teams get value out of this critical concept.

The vast majority of times I meet a team that has been working hard to create an MVP I am able to convince them that they could have achieved the same learning in a fraction of the time and effort.

(continued)

(continued)

They have spent literally months building an MVP when they could have had this same learning in days or, sometimes, even in hours.

The other unhappy consequence is that very often the rest of the company—especially key leadership in sales and marketing—is confused and embarrassed by what the product team is trying to get customers to buy and use.

While this is partly a result of the way most people have learned this concept, I think the root of the issue is that while the P in MVP stands for *product*, an MVP should *never* be an actual product (where product is defined as something that your developers can release with confidence, that your customers can run their business on, and that you can sell and support).

The MVP should be a *prototype*, not a product.

Building an actual product-quality deliverable to learn, even if that deliverable has minimal functionality, leads to substantial waste of time and money, which of course is the antithesis of Lean.

I find that using the more general term *prototype* makes this critical point clear to the product team, the company, and the prospective customers.

So, in this book, I talk about different types of *prototypes* being used in discovery and *products* being produced in delivery.

II

The Right People

Every product begins with the people on the cross-functional product team. How you define the roles, and the people you select to staff the team, will very likely prove to be a determining factor in its success or failure.

This is an area in which many companies fall short, stuck in old models of the past. For many organizations, the roles and responsibilities discussed here represent significant differences from what they're used to.

In Part Two, I describe the key roles and responsibilities of modern technology-powered product teams.

Product Teams

Overview

This is probably the most important concept in this entire book:

It's all about the product team.

You'll hear me say this many different ways throughout the chapters to follow, but so much of what we do in a strong product organization is to optimize for the effectiveness of product teams.

CHAPTER 9

Principles of Strong
Product Teams

In later chapters, I explore each of the key roles on a team, but in this chapter, I explain the principles of a strong product team.

Product teams are sometimes referred to as a *dedicated product team* or as a *durable product team*, to emphasize that these are not created just to work on a single project or feature, or sometimes as a *squad*—derived from the military analogy and meant to emphasize that these are cross-functional teams.

A product team is a group of people who bring together different specialized skills and responsibilities and feel real ownership for a product or at least a substantial piece of a larger product.

There are many ways to set up product teams (we'll discuss these later in the section People @ Scale). But in good product companies, you'll find that, despite the differences due to their unique products and circumstances, there are several very important similarities.

Team of Missionaries

There are many benefits of product teams, but a big goal is captured best by a quote from John Doerr, the famous Silicon Valley venture capitalist: "We need teams of missionaries, not teams of mercenaries."

Mercenaries build whatever they're told to build. *Missionaries* are true believers in the vision and are committed to solving problems for their customers. In a dedicated product team, the team acts and feels a lot like a startup within the larger company, and that's very much the intention.

> *We need teams of missionaries, not teams of mercenaries.*

Team Composition

A typical product team is comprised of a product manager, a product designer, and somewhere between two and about 10 to 12 engineers.

Of course, if the product you're working on doesn't have a user-facing experience—such as for a set of programmatic APIs—you probably don't need the product designer. But many product teams do need this person on board, and throughout this book, I'll generally assume your team does, too.

Teams might also have a few other members such as a product marketing manager, one or more test automation engineers, a user researcher, a data analyst, and, in larger product organizations, a delivery manager.

Don't worry if you don't yet know what some of these roles are—we'll soon explore each of them.

Team Empowerment and Accountability

A big part of the concept of product teams is that they are there to solve hard problems for the business. They are given clear objectives, and they own delivering on those objectives.

They are empowered to figure out the best way to meet those objectives, and they are accountable for the results.

Team Size

There's no rule that says all product teams in a company need to be the same size. It's true there is the notion of critical mass for a product team—usually one product manager, one designer, and two engineers. However, some teams might justify five engineers and two test automation engineers—others even more.

There is a practical upper bound on a team, which usually works out to be around 8–12 engineers. You've probably heard about the *two-pizza rule*, which is intended to help keep teams in this range.

More important than the absolute size of the team is the balance of skills needed to ensure we build the right things, and build those things right.

Team Reporting Structure

Note that I haven't said anything yet about who works for whom.

A product team is not about reporting relationships—it has an intentionally flat organizational structure. Usually, everyone on a product team is an individual contributor, and there are no people managers.

The people on the team typically continue to report to their functional manager. For example, the engineers report to an engineering manager. Likewise, the designer usually reports to a head of design, and the product manager reports into a head of product. So, this is not about reporting relationships.

To be absolutely clear, the product manager is not the boss of *anyone* on the product team.

Team Collaboration

A product team is a set of highly skilled people who come together for an extended period of time to solve hard business problems.

The nature of the relationship is more about true collaboration. I don't mean collaboration as a buzzword, either. I literally mean product, design, and engineering working out solutions together. Much more on that to come, but at this point, it's important for you to understand that this is not a hierarchy.

Team Location

I also haven't said anything yet about where the members of the team are physically located. While this isn't always possible, we try very hard to *co-locate* this team.

Co-location means that team members literally sit right next to one another. That doesn't mean in the same building or even the same floor. It means close enough to easily see each other's computer screens.

I know this sounds a bit old school, and the tools for remote collaboration are getting better all the time, but the best companies have learned the value of sitting together as a team.

If you've ever been a member of a co-located product team, you likely already know what I mean. But, as you'll see from how we do our work on a product team, there is a special dynamic that occurs when the team sits together, eats lunch together, and builds personal relationships with one another.

I'm aware this can be a bit of an emotional topic. For personal reasons, quite a few people live somewhere other than where they work, and their livelihood depends on working effectively remotely.

I don't want to paint this as too black or white, but I also don't want to mislead you. All other things being equal, a co-located team is going to substantially outperform a dispersed team. That's just the way it is.

This is also one of the reasons why we greatly prefer members of a product team to be actual employees and not contractors or agencies. It's much easier to be co-located and to be a stable member of the team if the person is an employee.

Note that there is nothing wrong with a company having multiple locations, so long as we try hard to have co-located teams in each location.

We'll talk later about what we do when not all the members are able to sit together.

Team Scope

Once you've got the basics of a product team, the next big question is this: What is the scope or charter of each team? That is, what is each team responsible for?

One dimension of this is the *type of work* to be done, and it's important that a product team has responsibility for all the work—all the projects, features, bug fixes, performance work, optimizations, and content changes—everything and anything for their product.

The other dimension is the *scope of work* to be done. In some types of companies, the product team is responsible for a complete product. But it's more common today that the product is the full customer experience (imagine a Facebook or a PayPal), and each team is responsible for some smaller but meaningful piece of that experience.

For example, you might be working on a team at eBay that's responsible for technology to detect and prevent fraud or tools and services for high-volume sellers. Or, at Facebook, your team might be responsible for newsfeeds, an iOS native mobile app, or the capabilities required for a specific vertical market.

This is an easy topic for a small startup, as you typically just have one or a small number of teams, which makes it relatively easy to split things up.

But as a company grows, the number of teams expands from a handful to 20, 50, or more teams in large product companies. The coordination gets harder (much more on that when we get to the section on Product @ Scale), but the concept is highly scalable and, in fact, is one of the keys to scalability.

There are lots of useful ways to slice up the pie. Sometimes we have each team focus on a different type of user or customer. Sometimes each team is responsible for a different type of device. Sometimes we break things up by workflow or customer journey.

Sometimes, actually very often, we are largely defining the teams based on the architecture. This is pretty common because the architecture drives the technology stack, which often requires different types of engineering expertise.

In any case, what's critically important is alignment between product management and engineering. This is why the head of product and the head of engineering normally get together to define the size and scope of the teams.

I will tell you there's never a perfect way to carve up the pie. Realize that, when you optimize for one thing, it comes at the expense of something else. So, decide what's most important to you and go with that.

Team Duration

I've mentioned a few times already that these teams need to be durable, but I haven't said whether this means for a few months or several years.

The bottom line is that we try hard to keep teams together and fairly stable.

While things do come up, and people change jobs and teams, once the members of a team get to know one another, and learn how to work well together, it's honestly a beautiful and powerful thing, and we try hard not to mess up that dynamic.

Another reason that durability is important is that it can take some time to gain enough expertise in an area to innovate. If people are moving from team to team all the time, it's hard for them to get that expertise and to feel the necessary sense of ownership over their product and missionary-like passion.

And to be clear, a product team is not something we create just to deliver a specific *project*. It's nearly impossible to have a team of missionaries when they're pulled together for a project that lasts only a few months and is then disbanded.

Team Autonomy

If we want teams to feel empowered and have missionary-like passion for solving customer problems, we need to give them a significant degree of autonomy. Obviously, this doesn't mean they can go off and work on whatever looks fun, but it does mean that they are able to try to solve the problems they are assigned in the best way they see fit.

It also means we try to minimize dependencies between teams. Notice that I said "minimize" and not "eliminate." At scale, it's just not possible to eliminate all dependencies, but we can work hard to continuously minimize them.

> *They are able to try to solve the problems they are assigned in the best way they see fit.*

Why It Works

Product companies moved to this model several years ago, and it's now one of the pillars of modern, strong product organizations. There are several reasons why this model has been so effective.

First, collaboration is built on relationships, and product teams—especially co-located teams—are designed to nurture these relationships.

Second, to innovate you need expertise, and the durable nature of product teams lets people go deep enough to gain that expertise.

Third, instead of just building what others determine might be valuable, in the product team model the full team understands—needs to understand—the business objectives and context. And most important, the full team feels ownership and responsibility for the *outcome*.

Instead of the old project-oriented model, which is all about getting something pushed through the process and out the door, in the dedicated team model, the team is not off the hook just because something launches. They don't rest until and unless it's working for the users and for the business.

Hopefully you're already a member of a strong, dedicated product team, and now you just have a better appreciation for the intention of this model.

On the other hand, if your company is not yet set up around dedicated product teams, this is probably the most important thing for you to fix. Everything else depends on this.

You don't have to move the whole organization there at once—you can start a team as a pilot. But one way or another, it's essential that you create or join a durable product team.

Principles and Techniques

I want to be clear as to why you'll see so many principles called out in this book.

When I coach product managers, I always try my best to explain the underlying principles of *why* we need to work the way we do.

(continued)

(continued)

I find that when a person reaches the point that they have a solid understanding of the principles, they develop a good mental model for when each technique is useful and appropriate, and when it is not. Further, as new techniques emerge, they are able to quickly assess the potential value of the technique, and when and where it is best utilized.

I have found over the years that while the techniques change fairly constantly, the underlying principles endure. So, while it may be tempting to jump right to the techniques, I hope you will first consider the principles, and work to develop a deeper understanding of how to build great products.

10

The Product Manager

This book is about becoming an excellent product manager, and in this chapter, I want to be very explicit about what that really means. But first, it's time for a little dose of tough love.

There are essentially three ways for a product manager to work, and I argue only one of them leads to success:

1. **The product manager can escalate every issue and decision up to the CEO.** In this model, the product manager is really a *backlog administrator*. Lots of CEOs tell me this is the model they find themselves in, and it's not scaling. If you think the product manager job is what's described in a *Certified Scrum Product Owner* class, you almost certainly fall into this category.

2. **The product manager can call a meeting with all the stakeholders in the room and then let them fight it out.** This is design by committee, and it rarely yields anything beyond mediocrity. In this model, very common in large companies, the product manager is really a *roadmap administrator*.

3. **The product manager can do his or her job.**

My intention in this book is to convince you of this third way of working. It will take me the entire book to describe how the strong product manager does his or her job, but let me just say for now

> *The honest truth is that the product manager needs to be among the strongest talent in the company.*

that this is a very demanding job and requires a strong set of skills and strengths.

The reason for calling this out so bluntly is that, in many companies, especially older, enterprise companies, the product manager role has a bad reputation. What too often happens is that the company takes people from other organizational roles—often project management or sometimes business analysts—and they say, "We're moving to Agile and we don't need project managers or business analysts anymore, so we need you to be a product manager."

The honest truth is that the product manager needs to be among the strongest talent in the company. If the product manager doesn't have the technology sophistication, doesn't have the business savvy, doesn't have the credibility with the key executives, doesn't have the deep customer knowledge, doesn't have the passion for the product, or doesn't have the respect of their product team, then it's a sure recipe for failure.

There are lots of ways to describe this particular role. Some people prefer to focus on the raw ingredients of what makes a strong product manager. Others tend to focus on the product manager's day-to-day activities and what they'll be spending their time doing.

We'll cover all that, but to me what's most important to talk about is what product managers are responsible for contributing to their team. That's not so obvious for the product manager. It's not that unusual for people to question whether they even need a product manager. If they don't design and they don't code, why bother?

This is a clear sign of a company that hasn't experienced strong product management.

Key Responsibilities

At one level, the responsibilities of the product manager are pretty straightforward. He or she is responsible for evaluating opportunities and determining what gets built and delivered to customers. We generally describe what needs to get built on the product *backlog*.

Sounds simple enough. And the mechanics of that are not the hard part. What's hard is to make sure that what goes on the product

> *When a product succeeds, it's because everyone on the team did what they needed to do. But when a product fails, it's the product manager's fault.*

backlog is worth building. And, today, on the best teams, the engineers and designers want to see some *evidence* that what you're asking to build is truly worth building.

But if you want to know why the product manager role is considered so important today by CEOs and venture capitalists (VCs), it's this:

Every business depends on customers. And what customers buy—or choose to use—is your product. The product is the result of what the product team builds, and the product manager is responsible for what the product team will build.

So, this is why the product manager is the person we hold responsible and accountable for the success of the product.

When a product succeeds, it's because everyone on the team did what they needed to do. But when a product fails, it's the product manager's fault.

You can start to see why this role is a proving ground for future CEOs and why the best VCs only want to invest in a company that has one of these proven product people as one of the co-founders.

So, this chapter is really about what you need to do to succeed at this job. In that spirit, there are four key responsibilities of a strong product manager; four things that the rest of your team is counting on you to bring to the party:

Deep Knowledge of the Customer

First and foremost is deep knowledge of the actual users and customers. To make this explicit, you need to become an acknowledged expert on the customer: their issues, pains, desires, how they think—and for business products, how they work, and how they decide to buy.

This is what informs so many of the decisions that must be made every day. Without this deep customer knowledge, you're just guessing. This requires both qualitative learning (to understand *why* our users and customers behave the way they do), and quantitative learning (to understand what they are doing), which is what we'll talk about next.

It should go without saying as it's really table stakes for a product manager, but just to be clear, the product manager must also be an undisputed expert on your actual product.

Deep Knowledge of the Data

Today, product managers are expected to be comfortable with data and analytics. They are expected to have both quantitative skills as well as qualitative skills. The Internet enables unprecedented volume and timeliness of data.

A big part of knowing your customer is understanding what they're doing with your product. Most product managers start their day with half an hour or so in the analytics tools, understanding what's been happening in the past 24 hours. They're looking at sales analytics and usage analytics. They're looking at the results of A/B tests.

You might have a data analyst to help you with this, but the analysis of the data and understanding you get of your customer is not something you can delegate.

Deep Knowledge of Your Business

Successful products are not only loved by your customers, but they work for your business.

The third critical contribution—and the one that is often considered the most difficult by many product managers—is a deep understanding of *your* business and how it works, and the role your product plays in your business. This is tougher than it sounds.

> *Successful products are not only loved by your customers, but they work for your business.*

This means knowing who your various stakeholders are and especially learning the constraints they operate under. There are usually key stakeholders representing general management, sales, marketing, finance, legal, business development, and customer service. Your CEO is usually a very important stakeholder as well.

Succeeding in the job of product means convincing each key stakeholder that you understand their constraints and that you are committed to only delivering solutions that you believe are consistent with those constraints.

Deep Knowledge of Your Market and Industry

The fourth critical contribution is deep knowledge of the market and industry in which you're competing. This includes not only your competitors but also key trends in technology, customer behaviors and expectations, following the relevant industry analysts, and understanding the role of social media for your market and customers.

Most markets have more competitors today than ever before. Further, companies understand the value in making products that are sticky, and this means that it can be difficult for prospective customers to move from your competitor to you. This is one of the big reasons why it is not enough to have feature parity with a competitor. Rather, you need to be *substantially better* to motivate a user or customer to switch.

Another reason to have a deep understanding of the competitive landscape is that your products will need to fit into a more general ecosystem of other products, and ideally your product is not only compatible with that ecosystem but adds significant value to it.

Further, your industry is constantly moving, and we must create products for where the market will be tomorrow, not where it was yesterday.

As an example, as of this writing, there is a major enabling technology trend sweeping through our industry, which is based on machine learning and other forms of artificial intelligence. I feel comfortable predicting that this will be a major technology trend for at least the next decade, and this is why you need to love technology-powered products. What is possible is constantly changing. If you're not excited about learning these new technologies, and exploring with your engineers and designers how you can use these trends to deliver dramatically improved products and experiences to your customers, then you really need to consider whether this career is for you.

To summarize, these are the four critical contributions you need to bring to your team: deep knowledge (1) of your customer, (2) of the data, (3) of your business and its stakeholders, and (4) of your market and industry.

If you're a designer or engineer, and you've been asked to cover the product manager role as well, then this is what you need to sign up for. I warned you—it's a ton of work.

One additional note: In some companies, there is so much in terms of industry and domain knowledge that the product manager may be supplemented with what are called *domain experts* or *subject matter experts*. Examples of domain experts can be found in companies that build tax software or create medical devices. In these cases, you can't expect the product managers to have the necessary level of domain depth, in addition to everything else. But these cases are fairly rare. The normal case is that the product manager does need to have (or be able to learn) the necessary domain expertise.

It normally takes about two to three months of dedicated work for a new product manager to get up to speed. This assumes you have a manager who can give you the help and access you need to gain this expertise, including lots of access to customers, access to data (and when necessary, training in the tools to access that data), access to key stakeholders, and time to learn your product and industry inside and out.

Smart, Creative, and Persistent

Now that we've seen what the product manager needs to contribute to the team, let's consider the kind of person who thrives in this environment.

The successful product manager must be the very best versions of *smart*, *creative*, and *persistent*.

By smart, I don't just mean raw IQ. I especially mean intellectually curious, quickly learning and applying new technologies to solve problems for customers, to reach new audiences, or to enable new business models.

> *The successful product manager must be the very best versions of* smart, creative, *and* persistent.

By creative, I mean thinking outside the normal product box of features to solve business problems.

By persistent, I mean pushing companies way beyond their comfort zone with compelling evidence, constant communication, and building bridges across functions in the face of stubborn resistance.

The passion for products and for solving customer problems is not something I think you can teach. That's something you either have or don't have, and it is among the first things I interview for when I'm evaluating potential product managers. I assume that *you* have this.

Maybe this is a good time to be very honest with you about the demands of this role.

The product manager position is not a 9-to-5 job. I'm not saying you need to be in the office 15 hours a day, but I am saying that there is a ton of work, and it follows you home every night. Pretty much any other role on a product team is better if you're looking for a good work-life balance. Now, I know it may not be politically correct to say that, but I don't think I'm doing you any favors by misleading you. The level of time and effort required by the product manager role is extremely tough to sustain if you're not personally passionate about your products and your role.

Perhaps the most important thing I can tell you to help you succeed is that you simply must take very seriously your preparation for this role.

- Start by becoming an expert in your users and customers. Share very openly what you learn, both the good and the bad. Become your team's and your company's go-to person for understanding anything about your customer—quantitative and qualitative.

- Work to establish a strong relationship with your key stakeholders and business partners. Convince them of two things: (1) You understand the constraints they operate under. (2) You will only bring to them solutions that you believe will work within those constraints.
- Become an undisputed expert on your product and your industry. Again, share your knowledge openly and generously.
- Finally, work very hard to build and nurture the strong collaborative relationship with your product team.

I'm not saying that doing all this is easy; it's not. But believe me when I tell you it's table stakes for being a successful product manager.

Product Manager Profiles

In addition to giving you the theory and techniques in this book, I make a point of introducing you to real people—product managers who have done their job and done it well. These individuals include:

- Jane Manning of Google
- Lea Hickman of Adobe
- Alex Pressland of the BBC
- Martina Lauchengco of Microsoft
- Kate Arnold of Netflix
- Camille Hearst of Apple

Anyone who's ever worked in product for any amount of time knows that creating products is never easy. I selected these particular individuals to illustrate the very difficult but essential contribution that comes from a strong product manager.

The products I highlight are all iconic, and you will immediately recognize them. But few people know the product managers behind these products, and even fewer know their backstories.

Each of the product managers I selected went out of her way to emphasize to me just how amazing their product team was, and how in no way was the success due to their efforts alone. But hopefully these examples help make clear to you the true and essential contribution of the product manager.

The big points I hope you take away from these examples are:

1. **Product management is absolutely distinct from the other disciplines.** It's clearly different than the contribution of the designers, and it's also clearly not a project manager. There is some amount of project management inevitably involved, just as there is for all leadership positions. But to characterize this as a project manager is to completely miss the essence of the role. The role I would argue the product manager is most similar to is the role of the CEO. But with the obvious difference that, unlike the CEO, the product manager is not the boss of anyone.

2. **Like a CEO, the product manager must deeply understand all aspects of the business.** The product manager must ensure a business outcome, not just ensure a product gets defined. This requires a good understanding of the many interrelated parts and constraints of the business—financial, marketing, sales, legal, partnership, service, the customer environment, the technical capabilities, the user's experience—and figure out a solution that works for the customers as well as for the business. But don't think this means an MBA is required—not one of the impressive product managers I feature in this book has an MBA—or that you need to have all these skills yourself. You must simply have a broad understanding of how a product can affect a business and work with people from your team and across your company to cover everything that's important.

3. **In every one of these examples, the winning solutions didn't come from users, customers, or sales.** Rather, great products require an intense collaboration with design and engineering to solve real problems for your users and customers, in ways that meet the needs of your business. In each of these examples, the users had no idea the solution they fell in love with was possible.

4. **True leadership is a big part of what separates the great product people from the merely good ones.** So, no matter what your title or level may be, if you aspire to be great, don't be afraid to lead.

> *No matter what your title or level may be, if you aspire to be great, don't be afraid to lead.*

Product Manager versus Product Owner

You've likely encountered the term *product owner*, and you may wonder how it relates to the product manager job.

First, product owner is the name of the *role* on an Agile team for the person responsible for the product backlog. Keep in mind that Agile is used in all types of companies, not just product companies.

In product companies, it is critical that the product manager also be the product owner. If you split these roles into two people, some very common and predictable problems

> *In product companies, it is critical that the product manager also be the product owner.*

result—most commonly, the loss of your team's ability to innovate and consistently create new value for your business and your customers. Moreover, the additional responsibilities of the product manager are what enables good product owner decisions in a product company.

Second, while I always encourage product managers to learn the development process their team is using, taking a class or certification on the product owner role covers a very small part of the responsibilities of a product manager.

To summarize, product owner responsibilities are a small subset of product management responsibilities, but it's critical that the product manager covers both.

The Two Critical Classes for Product Managers

Product managers come to the role from any and all disciplines. Certainly, many come from computer science, while others may come from business or economics. But you'll find great product managers that come from politics, philosophy, art, literature, history—and everything in between.

If you want to be an engineer or a designer, there is an academic education to be had that will prepare you for a career in those fields. That is not the case with tech product management. That's because what's most essential for this job is the smart, creative, and persistent qualities I've discussed.

That said, I believe there are two specific academic courses that every product manager should take:

1. **Introduction to Computer Programming**

   If you have never taken a course in a programming language, then this is your first necessary class. It doesn't really matter which language but not HTML. You can try to do this online, but I will tell you that many people struggle with learning their first programming language; therefore, an actual course for which you're accountable for turning in programming assignments every week is what it usually takes.

   You may love it, or you may hate it, but either way it will fundamentally expand your technology horizons and enable you to have much richer discussions with your engineers and designers. It will also give you a better appreciation for the power of enabling technology.

2. **Introduction to Business Accounting/Finance**

   Just as you need to know the language of computing, you also need to know the language of business. If you have never done so, you need to take a course in the basics of business finance.

   (continued)

(continued)

You will need to understand how for-profit companies work and the main business key performance indicators (KPIs) that are important to your business—including, but not limited to, lifetime value of customers, average revenue per user/customer, customer acquisition cost, cost of sales, and contribution margins, among others.

A good general marketing course will often cover these topics as well. The key is to make sure you gain a big-picture understanding of how businesses work.

You can easily do this through a community college course or through self-study, especially if you ask someone in your finance department to guide you a little. This is a good thing to do in any case.

The Product Designer

In this chapter, I describe the product designer role. But I'm not trying to speak here to designers—I'm aiming this at product managers who need to learn how to work effectively with designers.

It's amazing to me how many companies I encounter that just don't understand why having strong and talented designers is so important. They understand the need for engineers, but often will waste significant time and money because they do not understand the need for design.

Modern product designers are responsible for the following:

Product Discovery

In the old model, designers took requirements or specifications from product managers and used that to create their designs. In contrast, modern product designers continuously collaborate with product managers and engineers—from discovery to delivery. Similarly, rather than sitting with fellow designers, the modern product designer sits side by side with his or her product manager, a full partner with the product manager on product discovery.

Rather than being measured on the output of their design work, the product designer is measured on the success of the product. Given this, product designers have many of the same concerns as product managers. They are deeply oriented around actual customers and the

> *Rather than being measured on the output of their design work, the product designer is measured on the success of the product.*

value their product brings to those customers. They also understand that the product is in service of a business and can incorporate those constraints into the design of the product. Designers further understand that the user experience is as important to customer value as is the underlying functionality.

Holistic User Experience Design

User experience (UX) is much bigger than user interface (UI). Some people even use the term *customer experience* to further emphasize the point. UX is any way that customers and end users realize the value provided by your product. It includes all the touch points and interactions a customer has with your company and product over time. For modern products, this usually includes multiple different interfaces, as well as other customer touch points (e-mail, marketing campaigns, sales process, customer support, and so forth).

With some products, UX also includes offline services, such as riding in a car summoned through Uber or staying in a house sourced through Airbnb.

Good product designers think about the customer's journey over time as they interact with the product and with the company as a whole. Depending on the product, the list of touch points could be very long, considering questions as:

- How will customers first learn about the product?
- How will we onboard a first-time user and (perhaps gradually) reveal new functionality?

- How might users interact at different times during their day?
- What other things are competing for the user's attention?
- How might things be different for a one-month-old customer versus a one-year-old customer?
- How will we motivate a user to a higher level of commitment to the product?
- How will we create moments of gratification?
- How will a user share his experience with others?
- How will customers receive an offline service?
- What is the perceived responsiveness of the product?

Prototyping

Later in this book I explore the many techniques used to test out product ideas. Many of these techniques depend on prototypes, and most of these prototypes are created by the product designer.

Good product designers use prototypes as their primary canvas for communicating ideas, both internally and externally. They are generally comfortable with many different prototyping tools and are able to apply the correct one for the task at hand.

User Testing

Good product designers are constantly testing their ideas with real users and customers. They don't just test when a prototype or idea is ready; they build testing into their weekly cadence, so they're able to constantly validate and refine ideas as well as collect new insights they might not have been looking for. It also means that they aren't as likely to become too attached to ideas before they come in contact with objective, outside opinions.

User testing is broader than usability testing. Product designers and their product teams utilize the opportunity to assess the *value* of their ideas. Will customers use or buy the product and, if not, why not?

Interaction and Visual Design

Interaction and visual design have historically been considered separate roles. *Interaction design* generally includes the underlying conceptual models (e.g., a photo management application may have photos, albums, projects), task flows, and control layouts to manipulate those concepts. *Visual design* includes composition, typography, and how the visual brand is expressed.

Modern product designers may have different strengths but, generally, have some level of skill with both interaction and visual design. Having a more complete tool set allows them to work quickly at different levels of fidelity, depending on the context. It also allows them to design experiences in ways that wouldn't have been natural when thinking of interaction and visual design separately. This is particularly important in mobile interfaces in which designers must often create new models of interaction fundamentally intertwined with the visual design.

If you're building devices such as consumer electronics, there's another critical dimension to design—*industrial design*—which looks at materials and design for manufacturing.

The Absence of Product Design

Three situations in particular are incredibly common and serious problems:

1. You as product manager try to do the actual design yourself. Now, this is distinct from the situation where you are a trained designer and have also taken on the product manager responsibilities. In this situation, you have *not* been trained in design; yet, your engineers clearly need designs, so you oblige. That usually means you provide the engineers with wireframes, and they cobble together some form of visual design themselves.

2. You as product manager don't provide the designs but, rather, provide very high-level user stories to the engineers. To begin coding, the engineers have no choice but to work out the design themselves.

3. You as product manager provide the interaction design—especially the wireframes—and then you use a visual or graphic designer to provide the visual design.

All three situations are serious problems because they rarely provide good results. They don't provide the full holistic design we're looking for.

Apple is one of the most valuable and design-conscious companies on the planet; yet few tech companies understand the importance of design talent. While everyone talks about the engineers at Google and Facebook—and their engineering is indeed strong—both companies have made huge investments in design talent.

If you are building user-facing products, it's critically important that you get a trained product designer for your team. If you're doing products for consumers, I would argue that strong design today is table stakes. If you're doing products for businesses, then this is one of your best competitive differentiators.

It's sad to say, but most products for businesses have awful design. They've been able to get away with this, however, because the user is so often not the customer—the one that buys. I'm happy to say that's now changing, and there's a new breed of B2B (business-to-business) companies that take design very seriously. They are displacing the old guard.

In the case of products for small businesses, the user is typically the buyer, so the bar is set as high as it is for consumer products.

But getting your organization to invest in design staff is only half of the solution.

Here's why.

Many organizations wake up one morning and suddenly realize design is important. So, they spend money to bring this talent in-house; yet, they set up the operation like it's an internal agency. You're supposed to bring your design requests to this group of designers—often sitting together in their own little studio—and when they're done, you get the results.

> *We need design—not just as a service to make our product beautiful—but to discover the right product.*

If that's the way we needed to work, we'd probably continue to use external agencies. But it's not. We need design—not just as a service to make our product beautiful—but to discover the right product.

In strong teams today, the design informs the functionality at least as much as the functionality drives the design. This is a hugely important concept. For this to happen, we need to make design a first-class member of the product team, sitting side by side with the product manager, and not a supporting service.

Once you get a designer dedicated to your product team, here are five keys to a successful and healthy relationship with your designer:

1. Do whatever you need to do to have your designer sit next to you.

2. Include your designer from the very inception of every idea.

3. Include your designer in as many customer and user interactions as possible. Learn about the users and customers together.

4. Fight your temptation to provide your designer with your own design ideas. Give your designer as much room as possible to solve the design challenges him or herself.

5. Encourage your designer to iterate early and often. The best way you can encourage this is to not get all nitpicky about design details with the very early iterations. More generally, encourage your designer to feel free not to just iterate on the particular design approach but to explore alternative solutions to the problem.

The bottom line is that you and your designer really are partners. You're there to discover the necessary product solutions together, and you each bring different and critical skills to the team.

CHAPTER

12

The Engineers

In this chapter, I describe the engineering role (also commonly known as *developers* or, in some circles, *programmers*). But as with the last chapter, I'm not trying to speak here to the engineers—I'm aiming this discussion at product managers who need to learn how to work effectively with engineers.

There's probably no more important relationship for a successful product manager than the one with your engineers.

If your relationship is strong, with mutual and sincere respect both ways, then the product manager job is great. If your relationship is not strong, your days as product manager will be brutal (and probably numbered). Therefore, this is a relationship worth taking very seriously and doing everything you can to nurture.

This strong relationship begins with *you*. You need to do your homework and bring to the team the knowledge and skills of good product management.

Engineers are typically smart and often skeptical by nature, so if you're bluffing, they likely won't be fooled. If you don't know something, it's much better to fess up and say you'll find out rather than try to bluster.

It's also hugely important that you have an actual appreciation for the demands and complexities of the engineering job. If you were

> *There's probably no more important relationship for a successful product manager than the one with your engineers.*

an engineer before or if you've studied computer science in school, you're probably in good shape. But if not, I want to strongly encourage you to take a class at a local community college or online education where you'll learn a programming language.

The purpose of developing this programming literacy is not so you start telling your engineers how to do their job but, rather, to significantly improve your ability to engage with and collaborate with your engineers. Less obviously, but at least as important, this knowledge will give you a much better appreciation for technology and the art of the possible.

It's also critical that you share very openly what you know about your customers—especially their pain—the data, and your business constraints. Your job is to bring this information to your team and then to discuss the various potential solutions to these problems.

There is nothing wrong with you bringing a strong point of view, but you must constantly demonstrate to your team that you're open minded, you know how to listen, and you want and need their help in coming up with the right product.

As a practical matter, you need to engage directly with your engineers every workday. There are typically two types of discussions going on each day. In the first type of discussion, you're soliciting their ideas and input for the items you're working on in discovery. In the second type of discussion, they're asking you clarifying questions on the items they're working on delivering to production.

Where a lot of product managers go sideways is in how they communicate with their engineers. Just as most product managers don't like it when an executive or stakeholder spells out exactly what they want you to build, engineers generally don't like it when you try to spell out how to build something. So, while it's good if you have a strong technology understanding, it's not good if you use that knowledge to try to do their jobs for them.

You want to give your engineers as much latitude as possible in coming up with the best solution. Remember, they are the ones who will be called in the middle of the night to fix issues if they arise.

One last thing to keep in mind: the morale of the engineers is very much a function of you as the product manager. It is your job to make sure they feel like *missionaries* and not *mercenaries*. You do this by involving them deeply in the customer pain you are trying to solve and in the business problems you face. Don't try to shelter them from this—instead, share these problems and challenges very openly with them. They will respect you more for it, and, in most cases, the developers will rise to the challenge.

The Tech Lead Role

There are, of course, many different types of engineers. Some focus on engineering the user experience (generally referred to as *front-end developers*), and some focus on specific technologies (for example, database, search, machine learning).

Similarly, as with most other roles, there is a career progression for engineers. Many go on to become senior engineers, and some go from there to principal engineer or architect roles. Others move into more of an engineering leadership path, which generally starts with the *tech lead* role (aka *dev lead*, or *lead engineer*).

In general, from the product management perspective, any senior engineer is helpful because of the broad knowledge he or she brings that pertains to what is possible. However, a tech lead not only has this knowledge—and is responsible for helping to share this knowledge with the other engineers on the team—but the tech lead also has an explicit responsibility to help the product manager and product designer discover a strong solution.

Not every engineer or even senior engineer wants to participate in discovery activities, and this is fine. What's not okay is to have a

(continued)

(continued)

team of engineers in which *none* of them wants to engage in discovery activities.

It is for this reason that the product manager and product designer work most closely with the tech lead. In some product teams, there may be more than one tech lead, which is all the better.

It's also worth pointing out that engineers often have different work styles, which is also true for many designers. The product manager needs to be sensitive to the best way to interact. For example, many product managers are happy to speak in front of a larger group, or even a group of senior executives, but many engineers or designers are not. It's important to be sensitive to this.

13

Product Marketing Managers

P roduct marketing managers are a little different from the other members of the product team. This is not because they are any less important, but because the product marketing manager is usually not a full-time, dedicated member of each product team.

Product marketing is most typically organized by customer-facing product, by target market, or sometimes by go-to-market channel, especially for more established companies (e.g., enterprise, vertical, mid-market). There are typically fewer product marketers than product teams, as such, they get spread across different product teams.

In the best tech product companies, product marketing plays an essential role in discovery, delivery, and, ultimately, go-to-market, which is why they are important members of the product team.

As you'll soon see, coming up with winning products is never easy. We need a product that our customers love, yet also works for our business. However, a very large component of what is meant by *works for our business* is that there is a real market there (large enough to sustain a

business), we can successfully differ-
entiate from the many competitors
out there, we can cost-effectively
acquire and engage new customers,
and we have the go-to-market
channels and capabilities required
to get our product into the hands
of our customers.

Product marketing is our
critical partner in this.

Modern product marketing
managers represent the market to
the product team—the positioning, the messaging, and a winning

*Modern product marketing
managers represent the
market to the product
team—the positioning, the
messaging, and a winning
go-to-market plan. They
are deeply engaged with the
sales channel and know
their capabilities,
limitations, and current
competitive issues.*

go-to-market plan. They are deeply engaged with the sales channel
and know their capabilities, limitations, and current competitive issues.

The nature of product marketing is a bit different, depending
on the type of business you have and how your product gets to
market. When you make products for businesses that are sold through
either a direct sales force or a channel sales organization, it is a very
significant and critical job to declare the positioning—by that we
mean the market position the product must occupy, in addition to the
messaging—digital/content assets, sales tools, and training that enable
sales to effectively sell.

If your company has a sales organization, and you don't have
a product marketing partner, then this responsibility likely falls on
you as product manager. This can easily become a full-time job. And
given the cost of the sales organization, it's really not an option to
ignore them. But, of course, if you're spending your day helping the
sales organization, who is figuring out the product for these people
to sell?

If your company sells directly to consumers, it becomes easy for
the marketing teams to focus on clicks and brand at the expense of
ensuring all the product work adds up to a successfully differentiated
market position. This is important to the long-term prospects of any
company but also brings more meaning into all the work the product
team does.

It is very much in your best interest to make sure you have a product marketing manager to work with, and it's absolutely worth your time to make sure you understand the market—and your product marketing colleague understands the product—well enough for each of you to be successful.

There are many important interactions throughout discovery and delivery, so it's worth making a special effort to develop and maintain a strong working relationship with your product marketing colleague. For example, ensuring the product team is getting good signal from a broad enough representation of the market. It also becomes important in the messaging and deciding on the go-to-market plan based on these early product signals.

Note here that I am talking about the modern definition of the product marketing role. I am not describing the old model wherein product marketing was responsible for defining the product, and product management was primarily responsible for working with engineering to deliver that product.

Having a strong product marketing partner does not diminish in any sense the product manager's responsibility for delivering a successful product. The best product marketing manager and product manager relationships understand their respective roles but realize they are essential to each other's success.

14

The Supporting Roles

So far, we've talked about your role as product manager, and we've also talked about the designers, engineers, and product marketing managers you'll be working with very closely every day.

But there are other people in supporting roles you'll also work with. These people will probably not be dedicated solely to your team, as they are typically assigned to a small number of other product teams.

Now, you might not have any of the people I'm about to describe available to you. It really depends on the size and type of organization you work at. If you're at a small startup, you very probably will have none of these roles, and you will need to cover these activities yourself. But if you're at a company that has some or all of these roles, I want you to know why they exist and, most important, how to make the best use of these people.

User Researchers

As you'll soon see when we talk about how we do product discovery, we are continuously doing two kinds of rapid learning and experimentation. One kind of learning is *qualitative*, and the other is *quantitative*.

Especially with the qualitative learning, some of our research is *generative*, which is understanding the problems we need to solve; and some of our research is *evaluative*, which is assessing how well our solutions solve the problem.

User researchers are trained in this range of qualitative techniques (and some of them are also trained on the quantitative techniques as well). They can help you find the right type of users, craft the right types of tests, and learn the most from each user or customer interaction.

The key to tapping into the real value that these user researchers can provide is to keep in mind that the learning must be *shared learning*. You need to witness the insights first hand. More on this when we talk about the principles of product discovery, but while I want you to appreciate what user research can help you with, I don't want you to think you can delegate to them to do the learning and then send you a report.

If your company does not have user researchers, then your product designer will typically pick up these responsibilities for your team.

Data Analysts

Similarly, for quantitative learning, data analysts help teams collect the right sort of analytics, manage data privacy constraints, analyze the data, plan live-data tests, and understand and interpret the results.

Sometimes, data analysts go by the name business intelligence (BI) analysts, and they're experts in the types of data that your business collects and reports. It is well worth making friends with your data analyst. So much of product work today is data driven, and these people can be real gold mines for you and your organization.

In some companies, especially those with a lot of data—such as larger consumer companies—this may be a full-time role dedicated to a specific product team. In this case, the data analyst would be sitting and working alongside the product manager and product designer.

Data analysts help teams collect the right sort of analytics, manage data privacy constraints, analyze the data, plan live-data tests, and understand and interpret the results.

If your company does not have any data analysts, then responsibility for this typically falls on the product manager. If this is the case, you'll probably need to plan to spend significant time diving deep into the data to understand your situation and make good decisions.

Test Automation Engineers

Test automation engineers write automated tests for your product. They have largely replaced the old-style manual quality assurance (QA) people.

Now, it's very possible that your engineers are responsible both for writing software and for writing these automated tests. If that's the case, then you probably won't have many test automation engineers. But most companies have a blended approach in which the engineers write some of the automated tests (e.g., the unit level tests), and the test automation engineers write the higher-level automated tests.

Whichever model your company has is typically up to the engineering leadership, which is fine. However, what's not okay is if your company doesn't have test engineers, and your engineers don't do the testing either, and they are looking to you as product manager to do the quality testing.

While it's true as product manager you want to make sure things are generally as you expect before things go live (acceptance testing), that's a far cry from being able to release with confidence. The level of test automation necessary to release with confidence is significant and a big job. It's not unusual in complex products to have multiple test engineers dedicated to each product team.

15

Profile: Jane Manning of Google

I'm sure you have heard of Google's AdWords, and you may have also heard that this product is what fuels the Google empire. To be specific, as of this writing, AdWords is currently 16 years old, and in the most recent year alone, it generated well over *$60B in revenue*.

Yes, that's *B* as in *billions*.

What I'm guessing most of you don't know, however, is just how this industry-defining product came to be. And especially how close this product came to never happening at all.

The year was 2000, and the hardest part about the AdWords project was simply getting an agreement to work on it. The core idea had support from Larry Page, but the idea immediately encountered some pretty strong resistance from both the ad sales team and the engineering team.

Jane Manning was a young engineering manager asked to serve as product manager for this effort to try to get it off the dime.

The new sales team, under Omid Kordestani, was off to a strong start selling keywords to large brands and placing the results at the top of the search results. These results were highlighted as an ad but still very prominent—much in the style that had been done in search results at other companies, including at Netscape where Omid came from. Sales was nervous that this idea of a self-service advertising platform would diminish the value of what the sales team was trying to sell (known as *cannibalization*).

And the engineers, who had been working so hard to provide highly relevant search results, were understandably very worried that users would be confused and frustrated by ads getting in the way of their search results.

Jane sat down with each of these people to get a deeper understanding of their concerns. Some were just plain uncomfortable with advertising. Others were worried about cannibalization. And yet others were concerned about potential user unhappiness.

Once Jane understood the constraints and concerns, she had the information she needed to advocate for a solution that she believed would address the issues, yet enable countless small businesses to get a much more effective advertising solution. Jane also was able to persuade one of Google's earliest and most respected engineers, Georges Harik, of the idea's potential, and he helped to bring along other engineers.

The product solution they ended up with placed the AdWords-generated ads to the side of the search results, so they wouldn't be confused with the salesperson-sold ads, which were displayed on the top of the results.

Also, instead of determining placement based solely on the price paid, they would use a formula that multiplied the price paid per impression with the ad's performance (click-through-rate) to determine placement, so that the best-performing ads—the ones most likely to be most relevant to users—would rise to the top, and the worst ads would be unlikely to be displayed at all, even if they were sold at a higher price.

This solution clearly differentiated for the sales team and ensured quality search results, whether paid or organic.

Jane led the product discovery work and wrote the first spec for AdWords. Then she worked side by side with the engineers to build and launch the product, which was hugely successful.

This is yet another example of how there are always so many good reasons for products *not* to get built. In the products that succeed, there is always someone like Jane, behind the scenes, working to get over each and every one of the objections, whether they're technical, business, or anything else.

Jane took a break to start a family and is now back at Google once again, this time helping out the YouTube team.

This is yet another example of how there are always so many good reasons for products not to get built. In the products that succeed, there is always someone like Jane, behind the scenes, working to get over each and every one of the objections, whether they're technical, business, or anything else.

People @ Scale

Overview

Most companies know that they need to double down on their efforts to recruit very strong staff as they grow, but they don't always know what other changes are important as they grow and scale.

What are the changes in the leadership roles? How do we maintain the holistic view of product when we have many teams? How do we keep teams feeling empowered and autonomous when they just own a small part of the whole? How do we encourage accountability when the only person that owns everything is the CEO? How do we deal with the explosion of dependencies?

These are the topics we will tackle as we discuss how strong product organizations scale.

16

The Role of Leadership

The primary job of leadership in any technology organization is to recruit, to develop, and to retain strong talent. However, in a product company, the role goes beyond people development and into what we call *holistic view of product*.

For a startup, there's typically just one or two product teams, so it's not too hard for everyone to keep in their heads a holistic view of the product. However, this quickly becomes much tougher as the company grows—first to a larger product and soon to many product teams.

> *One of the big challenges of growth is knowing how the whole product hangs together. Some people like to think of holistic view as connecting the dots between the teams.*

One of the big challenges of growth is knowing how the whole product hangs together. Some people like to think of holistic view as connecting the dots between the teams.

The three distinct but critical elements to the holistic view of product are described next.

Leaders of Product Management

To ensure a holistic view of how the entire system fits together from a business point of view (product vision, strategy, functionality, business rules, and business logic), we need either the leaders of the product management organization (VP product, directors of product), or a principal product manager.

This person should regularly review the work of the various product managers and product teams, identifying and helping to resolve conflicts.

For large-scale organizations, some companies prefer this to be an individual contributor role (e.g., a principal product manager), but let me be clear that this is a very senior role (usually equivalent to a director-level manager). Since the head of product is first and foremost responsible for building the skills of the product managers, a dedicated principal product manager is able to focus on the *product* itself and is readily accessible as a critical resource to all the product managers, product designers, engineers, and test automation staff.

If you use a principal product manager for this, he or she should be a direct report to the head of product so that everyone understands the importance of the role and the responsibilities of that person.

Whether this role is covered by the head of product or a principal product manager, this is a critically essential role for companies with large and complex business systems, especially with many legacy systems.

Leaders of Product Design

One of the most important roles in a company is the person or people responsible for the holistic user experience. These leaders must ensure a consistent and effective user experience systemwide. This is sometimes the leader of the product design team, sometimes one of the managers or directors of design, and sometimes a principal designer reports to this leader. In any case, it must be someone very strong in holistic product design.

There are so many interactions and interdependencies—and so much necessary institutional knowledge of the business and the users and the customer journey—that at least one person must review everything going on with the product that is going to be visible to the user. You can't expect any individual product manager or designer to be able to have this all in their head.

Leaders of Technology Organization

Finally, to ensure a holistic view of how the entire system fits together from a technology point of view, we have a *technology organization leader* (often titled CTO or VP engineering). In practice, that person is often helped by a group of engineering managers and directors and/or software architects.

The CTO, managers, and architects are responsible for the holistic view of the system implementation. They should be reviewing the architecture and systems design of all the software—both systems developed by your own staff, as well as any systems designed by vendors. They should also have a clear strategy for managing technical debt.

Again, this is a critically essential role for companies with large and complex business systems, especially with many legacy systems, and should be placed in the organization somewhere that makes these people visible and available to the entire technology organization (this is usually a direct report to the head of technology).

Holistic View Leadership Roles

The larger the company gets, the more critical these three roles are, and their absence is usually all too obvious. If the product or site looks like it was created by half a dozen different outside design agencies, with conflicting user models and poor usability, you're probably missing a head of design or principal designer.

If projects are constantly getting stuck because product managers don't understand the implications of their decisions or product managers are constantly asking developers to look at the code to tell them how the system really works, then you're probably missing a principal product manager.

And if your software is a big mess of spaghetti and it takes forever to make even simple changes, you're probably suffering from significant technical debt.

You might ask what happens if one of these people gets hit by a bus or leaves the company? First and foremost, don't lose these people! Take care of them and don't give them any reason to want to leave or feel like they need to become a manager to make more money.

Second, you should always be trying to develop more of these people, and each of them should have at least one person they're working to develop into a strong second. But they are a rare and incredibly valuable commodity, as this learning does not happen overnight.

Some companies think the answer to this is to try to document the system to the degree that everything is captured somehow in a way that members of the organization can all go to get the same sorts of answers for which they use the principal designer, principal product manager, and software architect.

I know a few organizations that have tried hard to achieve this, but I have never seen this succeed. The systems always seem to grow in complexity and size much faster than anyone can document, and with software, the definitive answer always lives in the source code itself (at least the current answer—not usually the rationale or the history).

One final note: These three holistic-view leaders—the head of product, the head of design, and the head of technology—are obviously very valuable individually, but in combination you can see their real power. This is why my personal preference is to have these three people sit very close to one another, sometimes in the same physical office.

CHAPTER 17

The Head of Product Role

I've written this chapter for three specific audiences:

1. If you are a CEO or executive recruiter and you're looking for a head of product, this chapter will give you a deeper understanding of what kind of person you should be seeking.
2. If you are currently leading a product organization, I'd like to offer this up as your key to success.
3. If you have aspirations of one day leading a product organization, this is a frank discussion of the skills you'll need to acquire.

In this chapter, I use the title *VP product* to refer to this position, but you'll also find titles ranging from director of product management to chief product officer. Whatever the title may be, I am referring here to your most senior product role in your company or business unit.

Organizationally, this role typically manages the product managers and product designers, sometimes the data analysts, and generally reports to the CEO. With some exceptions, it is important that this role be a peer to the CTO and the VP marketing.

I'll say right up front that this is a difficult role, and it is difficult to perform well. Those who do succeed in it make a dramatic difference for their companies. Great product leaders are highly valued and often go on to found their own companies. In fact, some of the best venture capitalists only invest in founders who have already proved themselves as great product leaders.

Competencies

Specifically, you are looking for someone who is proved to be strong in four key competencies: (1) team development, (2) product vision, (3) execution, and (4) product culture.

Team Development

The single most important responsibility of any VP product is to develop a strong team of product managers and designers. This means making recruiting, training, and ongoing coaching the top priority. Realize that developing

> *The single most important responsibility of any VP product is to develop a strong team of product managers.*

great people requires a different set of skills than developing great products, which is why many otherwise excellent product managers and designers never progress to leading organizations.

One of the worst things you can do is take one of your poor-performing people and promote them to this leadership position. I know that may sound obvious, but you'd be surprised how many execs reason, "Well, this person is not very strong, but he works well with people, and the stakeholders seem to like him, so maybe I'll make him the head of product and hire a strong individual contributor to backfill him." But how do you expect this poor performer to help develop his or her team into strong performers? And what message does this send to the organization?

For this position, you need to ensure you hire someone who has *proven* ability to develop others. They should have a track record of identifying and recruiting potential talent, and then working actively and continuously with those people to address their weaknesses and exploit their strengths.

Product Vision and Strategy

The product vision is what drives and inspires the company and sustains the company through the ups and downs. This may sound straightforward, but it's tricky. That's because there are two very different types of product leaders needed for two very different situations:

1. Where there is a CEO or a founder who is the clear product visionary
2. Where there is no clear product visionary—usually in situations where the founder has moved on

There are two very bad situations you may encounter related to product vision and strategy.

The first is when you have a CEO who is very strong at product and vision, but she wants to hire a VP product (or, more often, the board pushes her to hire a VP product), and she thinks she should be hiring someone in her own image—or at least visionary like her. The result is typically an immediate clash and a short tenure for the VP product. If this position looks like a revolving door, it's very possible that's what's going on.

The second bad situation is when the CEO is not strong at vision, but she also hires someone in her own image. This doesn't result in the clash (they often get along great), but it does leave a serious void in terms of vision, and this causes frustration among the product teams, poor morale across the company, and usually a lack of innovation.

The key here is that the VP product needs to *complement* the CEO. If you have a strong, visionary CEO, there may be some very strong VP product candidates that won't want the position because they know that, in this company, their job is primarily to execute the vision of the CEO.

One situation that unfortunately happens is when you have a visionary founder CEO, and she has a solid partner running product who is very strong at execution, but the founder eventually leaves and now the company has a problem because nobody is there to provide the vision for the future. It's generally not something a VP product can easily turn on and off, and even if they can, the rest of the company may not be willing to consider the product leader in this new light. This is why I generally prefer when the founders stay on at the company, even if they decide they want to bring in someone else as the CEO.

If you're wondering what to do when you have a CEO who *thinks* she's a strong visionary leader, but the rest of the company knows she's not, you need a very special head of product, one that is a strong visionary, but also has the ability and willingness to convince the CEO the vision was all her idea.

Execution

No matter where the vision comes from, all the great vision in the world doesn't mean much if you can't get the product idea into the hands of customers. You need a product leader who knows how to get things done and has absolutely proved her ability to do so.

There are many aspects that contribute to a team's ability to execute consistently, rapidly, and effectively. The product leader should be expert on modern forms of product planning, customer discovery, product discovery, and product development process, but execution also means that they know how to work effectively as part of an organization of your size.

The bigger the organization, the more critical it is that the person has proven, strong skills—especially in stakeholder management and internal evangelism. The product leader must be able to inspire and motivate the company and get everyone moving in the same direction.

Product Culture

Good product organizations have a strong team, a solid vision, and consistent execution. A *great* product organization adds the dimension of a strong product culture.

A strong product culture means that the team understands the importance of continuous and rapid testing and learning.

They understand that they need to make mistakes in order to learn, but they need to make them quickly and mitigate the risks. They understand the need for continuous innovation. They know that great products are the result of true collaboration. They respect and value their designers and engineers. They understand the power of a motivated product team.

A strong VP product will understand the importance of a strong product culture, be able to give real examples of her own experiences with product culture, and have concrete plans for instilling this culture in your company.

Experience

The amount of relevant experience, such as domain experience, will depend on your particular company and industry. But at a minimum, you are looking for someone with the combination of a strong technology background with an understanding of the economics and dynamics of your business and your market.

Chemistry

Last but certainly not least, everything previously discussed is still not enough. There is one more thing: Your product leader must be able to work well on a personal level with the other key execs, especially the CEO and CTO. It will not be fun for any of you if there isn't that personal connection. Make sure the interview process includes a long dinner with at least the CEO and CTO and probably the head of marketing and head of design. Be open and make it personal.

> ### The Group Product Manager Role
>
> There's a role in larger product organizations that I find especially effective. The role is titled *group product manager*, usually referred to as GPM.
>
> The GPM is a hybrid role. Part individual contributor and part first-level people manager. The idea is that the GPM is already
>
> *(continued)*

(continued)

a proven product manager (usually coming from a senior product manager title), and now the person is ready for more responsibility.

There are generally two career paths for product managers.

One is to stay as an individual contributor, which, if you're strong enough, can go all the way up to a *principal product manager*—a person who's an individual contributor but a rock-star performer and willing and able to tackle the toughest product work. This is a very highly regarded role and generally compensated like a director or even VP.

The other path is to move into functional management of the product managers (the most common title is *director of product management*) where some number of product managers (usually somewhere between 3 and 10) report directly to you. The director of product management is really responsible for two things. The first is ensuring his or her product managers are all strong and capable. The second is product vision and strategy and connecting the dots between the product work of the many teams. This is also referred to as *holistic view of product*.

But lots of strong senior product managers are not sure about their preferred career path at this stage, and the GPM role is a great way to get a taste of both worlds.

The GPM is the actual product manager for one product team, but in addition, she is responsible for the development and coaching of a small number of additional product managers (typically, one to three others).

While the director of product management may have product managers who work across many different areas, the GPM model is designed to facilitate tightly coupled product teams.

This is easiest to explain with an example.

Let's say you're a growth stage marketplace company, and you have roughly 10 product teams. You may likely have those 10 teams split up into three types: a platform/common services group, and then a group for each side of the marketplace (e.g., buyers and sellers, riders and drivers, or hosts and guests).

(continued)

(continued)

There might be one VP product and three GPMs—one for each of the three groups, for example, a GPM of buyer side, a GPM of seller side, and a GPM of platform services.

So now let's drill in on the GPM for buyer side, and let's say there are three product teams comprising the buyer-side experience. The GPM of buyer side would have one of those teams, and each of the other two teams would have a product manager that reports to the GPM.

We like this because the buyer side really needs to be one seamless solution, even though there may be multiple product teams working on different aspects of it. The GPM works very closely with the other PMs to ensure this.

This role is often called a *player-coach* role because of this dynamic of leading your own team, in addition to being responsible for coaching and developing one to three other PMs.

Some GPMs go on to become a director or VP of product management, some go on to a principal product manager role, and some decide to stay on as a GPM because they love the blend of hands-on working with their own product team, as well as the ability to influence other teams and other product managers through coaching.

> *This role is often called a* player-coach *role because of this dynamic of leading your own team, in addition to being responsible for coaching and developing one to three other PMs.*

18

The Head of Technology Role

E ven with the greatest product ideas, if you can't build and launch your product, it remains just an idea. So, your relationship with the engineering organization is all important.

In this chapter, I describe the leader of the engineering organization. I had the good fortune to collaborate on this chapter with one of Silicon Valley's most successful CTOs, Chuck Geiger.

I have often said that, if as product manager you have a good working relationship with your engineering counterpart, then this is a great job. If you don't, you're in for some very tough days. So, in the spirit of developing a better appreciation for what makes a great technology organization, we offer this summary.

First, let's be clear which organization we're referring to. This is the organization responsible for architecture, engineering, quality, site operations, site security, release management, and usually delivery management. This group is responsible for building and running the company's products and services.

The titles vary but often include VP engineering, or chief technology officer (CTO). In this chapter, we'll refer to the head of this organization as the CTO, but feel free to substitute the term your company uses.

> *Even with the greatest product ideas, if you can't build and launch your product, it remains just an idea.*

There is one title, however, that is often a problem: the chief information officer (CIO). The CIO role is very different from the CTO role. In fact, if your technology organization reports to the CIO, that is a warning flag for many of the pathologies discussed in Chapter 6, "The Root Causes of Failed Product Efforts."

The hallmark of a great CTO is a commitment to continually strive for technology as a strategic enabler for the business and the products. Removing technology as a barrier, as well as broadening the art of the possible for business and product leaders, is the overarching objective.

To that end, there are six major responsibilities of a CTO. We present them here in priority order and discuss how each is typically measured.

Organization

Build an excellent organization with a strong management team committed to developing the skills of your employees. We typically measure effectiveness here by looking at development plans for all the employees, the retention rate, and the evaluation of the managers and the overall product and technology organization by the rest of the company.

Leadership

Represent technology in the overall strategic direction and leadership of the company, working with other company executives to help inform direction, M&A activity, and build/buy/partner decisions.

Delivery

Make sure this organization can rapidly, reliably, and repeatedly deliver quality product to market. There are several measures of delivery, including the consistency and frequency of release vehicles, and the quality/reliability of the delivered/launched software. The main obstacle to rapid delivery is often technical debt, and it is the responsibility of the CTO to ensure that the company is keeping this at a manageable level and not allowing the problem to cripple the organization's ability to deliver and compete, which is discussed next.

Architecture

Make sure the company has an architecture capable of delivering the functionality, scalability, reliability, security and performance it needs to compete and thrive. In companies that have multiple product lines or vertical business units, the CTO needs to be the leader in a cohesive technology strategy looking at the sum, and not just the parts. The CTO is the orchestrator of a company-wide technology strategy. The measures for architecture will vary based on your business, but in general, we look to ensure that the infrastructure is continuously monitored and advanced to keep pace with the growth of the business, and we measure outages that impact our customers that are due to infrastructure or architectural issues.

Discovery

Make sure that members of the senior engineering staff are participating actively and contributing significantly throughout product discovery. If your engineers and architects are only being used to write software, then you are only getting a fraction of the value from them you should be. We encourage you to keep an eye on the participation of the engineering organization in product discovery (both duration and coverage) and follow the frequency of innovations credited to the engineering participant.

Evangelism

The CTO will serve as the company spokesperson for the engineering organization, demonstrating leadership in the community with developers, partners, and customers. Leadership of this type can be measured by establishing a university relations/recruitment program and sponsoring or participating in several events per year in the developer community.

You may want to go to lunch with your engineering counterpart and discuss what they see as their biggest challenges and how you might be able to help from the product side. Anything you can do to help each other out will go a long way to creating a truly effective overall product organization, able to discover and deliver winning products.

19

The Delivery Manager Role

In growth-stage and enterprise companies, many product managers complain that they have to spend far too much of their time doing project management activities. As a result, they have almost no time to address their primary product responsibility: ensuring that the engineers have a product worth building.

Delivery managers are a special type of project manager whose mission is all about removing obstacles—also known as *impediments*—for the team. Sometimes, these obstacles involve other product teams, and sometimes they involve non-product functions. In a single day, they might track down someone in marketing and press them for a decision or an approval, coordinate with the delivery manager on another team about prioritizing a key dependency, persuade a product designer to create some visual assets for one of the front-end developers, and deal with a dozen other similar roadblocks.

These delivery managers are typically also the Scrum Masters for the team (if they have that role). They are all about helping the team to get stuff live faster, not by cracking the whip but by removing obstacles that get in the way.

These people might have the title project manager—or sometimes program manager—but if that's the case, then we need to make sure these people have defined the job like I did here and not in the old program management sense.

> *In growth-stage and enterprise companies, many product managers complain that they have to spend far too much of their time doing project management activities.*

If your company does not have delivery managers—by whatever title—then this work typically falls to the product manager and the engineering managers. Again, if your organization is small, then this is fine—and there are even advantages. But if your organization is larger—on the order of at least 5 to 10 product teams, then this role becomes increasingly important.

20

Principles of Structuring Product Teams

O ne of the most difficult issues facing every product organization at scale is just how to split up your product across your many product teams.

The need to split up your product starts to show up with just a few product teams, but at scale—25, 50, more than 100 product teams—this becomes a very substantial factor in the company's ability to move quickly. It's also a significant factor in keeping teams feeling empowered and accountable for something meaningful, yet contributing to a bigger vision where the sum is greater than the parts.

If you are already at scale, then I'm certain you know what I'm talking about.

What makes this such a difficult topic is that there is no one right answer. There are many considerations and factors, and good product companies debate the alternatives and then make a decision.

I have personally worked with many product and technology organizations as they considered the options, and for many of those, I've been able to watch how things worked out over time.

One of the most difficult issues facing every product organization at scale is just how to split up your product across your many product teams.

I know that many people crave a recipe for structuring product teams, but I always explain to them that there is no recipe. Instead, there are some critical core principles, and the key is to understand those principles and then weigh the options for your particular circumstances.

1. Alignment with investment strategy

   It's remarkable to me how many companies I find in which the teams are simply reflections of their ongoing investments. They have certain teams because they have always had those teams. But, of course, we need to be investing in our future as well. We can phase out products that no longer carry their own weight, and we can often reduce the investments in our cash-cow products so that we can invest more in future sources of revenue and growth. There are any number of ways to think about spreading out your investments over time and risk. Some people like the three horizons model, while others take more of a portfolio management approach. The point here is that you need to have an investment strategy, and your team structure should be a reflection of that.

2. Minimize Dependencies

   A big goal is to minimize dependencies. This helps teams move faster and feel much more autonomous. While we can never entirely eliminate dependencies, we can work to reduce and minimize them. Also note that dependencies change over time, so track them continuously and always ask yourself how they can be reduced.

3. Ownership and Autonomy

   Remember that one of the most important traits of product teams is that we want teams of missionaries and not teams of mercenaries. This leads directly to the concepts of ownership and autonomy. A team should feel empowered, yet accountable for some significant part of the product offering. This is harder than it sounds because large systems don't always slice up so cleanly. Some level of interdependencies will always chip away at the sense of ownership. But we work hard to try to maximize this.

4. Maximize Leverage

As organizations grow, we often find common needs and the increased importance of shared services. We do this for speed and reliability. We don't want every team reinventing the wheel. Realize, however, that creating shared services also creates dependencies and can impinge on autonomy.

5. Product Vision and Strategy

The product vision describes where we as an organization are trying to go, and the product strategy describes the major milestones to get there. Many larger and older organizations no longer have a relevant vision and strategy, but this is key. Once you have your vision and strategy, ensure you have structured the teams to be well positioned to deliver on them.

6. Team Size

This is a very practical principle. The minimum size for a product team is usually two engineers and a product manager, and if the team is responsible for user-facing technology, then a product designer is needed, too. Fewer than that is considered below critical mass for a product team. On the other end, it's really difficult for one product manager and product designer to keep more than about 10–12 engineers busy with good stuff to build. Also, in case it's not clear, it's important that each product team have one, and only one, product manager.

7. Alignment with Architecture

In practice, for many organizations the primary principle for structuring the product teams is the architecture. Many will start with the product vision, come up with an architectural approach to deliver on that vision, and then design the teams around that architecture.

That may sound backward to you, but in truth there are some really good reasons for this. Architectures drive technologies, which drive skill sets. While we'd love for every team to be a full stack team that can work on any layer of the architecture, in practice that's often not an option. Different engineers are trained in different technologies. Some want to specialize (and, in fact, have in many cases spent many years specializing), and some are years away from having the necessary skills. Architecture does not change quickly.

It's usually easy to see when a company has not paid attention to the architecture when they assemble their teams—it shows up a few different ways. First, the teams feel like they are constantly fighting the architecture. Second, interdependencies between teams seem disproportionate. Third, and really because of the first two, things move slowly, and teams don't feel very empowered.

For larger companies, especially, it's typical to have one or more teams that provide common services to the other product teams. We often label these teams *common services*, *core services*, or *platform* teams, but they primarily reflect the architecture. This is very high-high leverage, which is why so many companies have these types of teams at scale. However, it is also a difficult type of team to staff because these teams are dependencies (by design) of all the other teams, as they are there to *enable* the other teams. Be sure to staff these common services teams with strong and highly technical product managers (often called *platform product managers*).

8. Alignment with User or Customer

Aligning with the user and customer has very real benefits for the product and for the team. If, for example, your company provides a two-sided marketplace with buyers on one side and sellers on the other, there are real advantages to having some teams focus on buyers and others focus on sellers. Each product team can go very deep with *their* type of customers rather than have them try to learn about *all* types of customers. Even in marketplace companies, however, they will invariably have some number of teams that provide the common foundation and shared services to all the teams. This is really a reflection of the architecture, so the point here is that it is perfectly fine—and usual—to have both types of teams.

9. Alignment with Business

In larger companies, we often have multiple lines of business but a common foundation for our products. If the technology is truly independent across businesses, then we'd just treat them as essentially different companies as we structure product teams. However, mostly that's not the case. We have multiple lines of business, but all are built on a common and often integrated foundation. This is roughly similar to aligning by customer type, but there are important differences. Our business unit structure is an artificial construct. The different business units are often selling to the same actual customers. So, while there are advantages to aligning with business units, this usually comes after the other factors in priority.

10. Structure Is a Moving Target

Realize that the optimal structure of the product organization is a moving target. The organization's needs should and will change over time. It's not like you'll need to reorganize every few months, but reviewing your team structure every year or so makes sense.

I often have to explain to companies that there is never a perfect way to structure a team—every attempt at structuring the product organization will be optimized for some things at the expense of others. So, as with most things in product and technology, it involves tradeoffs and choices. My hope is that these principles will help you as you guide your organization forward.

Autonomy @ Scale

Most leading tech companies have jumped on the empowered, dedicated/durable, cross-functional, collaborative product team model I have described here, and I think they are much better for it.

(continued)

(continued)

The results speak for themselves, but I attribute most of the benefits to the increased level of motivation and true sense of ownership when teams feel more in control of their own destiny.

However, while most leaders tell me they have empowered, autonomous teams, some of the people on those teams complain to me that they don't always feel so empowered or autonomous. Whenever this happens, I try

> *I attribute most of the benefits to the increased level of motivation and true sense of ownership when teams feel more in control of their own destiny.*

to get to the specifics of just what it is that the team is not able to decide or where they feel constrained.

Most of what I hear falls into one of two cases:

1. In the first case, the team simply isn't trusted yet by management, and management is reluctant to give too long of a rope to the team.

2. In the second case, the team wants to change something that the leaders had assumed was part of the foundation.

In general, most teams would probably agree that there are some things that are wide open for the team to do as they think best and other areas that are part of the common foundation that all teams share.

As an example of the latter, it would be unusual for each team to select its own software configuration management tool. If the engineering team has standardized on GitHub, then that is usually considered part of the foundation. Even if one team had a strong preference for a different tool, the total cost to the organization of allowing its use would likely far outweigh any benefits.

While this might be a straightforward example, there are many others that are not so clear.

(continued)

(continued)

For example, should each team be able to approach test automation in its own way? Should teams be able to select the programming languages they wish to use? What about user interface frameworks? What about browser compatibility? How about expensive features like offline support? How about the flavor of Agile they wish to use? And does every team really need to support several company-wide product initiatives?

As is so often the case with product, things boil down to a tradeoff—in this case between the team's autonomy and leverage of the foundation.

I will also confess here that, while I love the core notion of autonomous, empowered teams, I am also a big fan of investing in a high-leverage foundation. This means building a strong foundation that all teams can leverage to create amazing products and experiences much faster than they would otherwise.

For the record, I do not believe that there is one answer to this question. The best answer is different for each company, and even for each team, and the best answer is also a function of the company's culture.

Here are the key factors to consider:

Team Skill Level

There are roughly three team skill levels: (1) A team—an experienced team that can be entrusted to make good choices; (2) B team—these people have the right intentions but may not have the level of experience necessary to make good decisions in many cases and may need some assistance; and (3) C team—this is a junior team that may not even know what they don't know yet. These teams can unintentionally cause substantial issues without significant coaching.

Importance of Speed

One of the main arguments for leverage is speed. The logic goes that teams should be able to build on the work of their colleagues

(continued)

(continued)

and not spend time reinventing the wheel. However, sometimes it's simply an accepted and acknowledged cost of empowerment to allow teams to potentially duplicate areas or proceed slower in the name of autonomy. Other times, the viability of the business depends on this leverage.

Importance of Integration

In some companies, the portfolio is a set of related, but largely independent, products in which integration and leverage is less important. In other companies, the portfolio is about a set of highly integrated products in which integration leverage is critical. This boils down to whether the team should optimize for its particular solution or optimize for the company as a whole.

Source of Innovation

If the main sources of future innovation are necessary at the foundation level, then there will need to be more freedom for teams to revisit core components. If the main sources of innovation are expected to be at the solution level, then the company needs to encourage less revisiting of the foundation and, instead, focus the creativity on application-level innovations.

Company Size and Locations

Many of the problematic issues with autonomy arise because of issues of scale. As companies grow, and especially as companies have teams in disperse locations, leverage becomes both more important and more difficult. Some companies try to deal with this with the *center of excellence* concept in which leverage is focused on teams in a physical location. Others try stronger holistic roles. Yet others add process.

Company Culture

It is also important to acknowledge the role that an emphasis on autonomy versus leverage plays in team culture. The further on the spectrum that the company pushes toward leverage, the more

(continued)

(continued)

this can be perceived by the teams as chipping away at their level of autonomy. This may be acceptable for B- and C-level teams but more problematic for A-level teams.

Maturity of Technology

One frequent problem is to try to standardize on a common foundation prematurely. The foundation isn't yet ready for prime time, in the sense of the leverage it is designed to provide. If you push too hard on leverage before the foundation is ready, you can truly hurt the teams that are counting on this foundation. You're building a house of cards that may collapse at any time.

Importance to Business

Assuming the foundation is solid, there's likely more risk in a team not leveraging that foundation. This might be fine for some areas, but with products or initiatives that are business critical, it becomes a question of which battles to pick.

Level of Accountability

Another factor is the level of accountability that goes along with the empowerment and autonomy. If there's no accountability—and especially if you don't have strong A teams—there's little reason for the teams to stress about these tradeoffs. But you *want* the teams to stress over these tradeoffs. If I believe the team is strong and they fully understand the consequences and risks, and yet they still feel they need to replace a key component of the foundation, then I tend to side with that team.

As you can see, there are no lack of considerations in the tradeoff between autonomy and leveraging the foundation. But, I find if you discuss these topics openly, most teams are reasonable. Sometimes, just a few key questions about some of the implications can help teams make better decisions regarding this tradeoff.

(continued)

(continued)

If you find that teams are consistently making poor decisions in this regard, you may need to consider the experience level of the people on the team, but most likely, the teams are missing the full business context.

The critical context is comprised of two things:

1. The overall product vision

2. The specific business objectives assigned to each team

We will discuss both of these key topics in the coming chapters. Problems arise if the leadership does not provide clarity on these two critical pieces of context. If they don't, there's a vacuum, and that leads to real ambiguity over what a team can decide and what they can't.

Note that while the product vision and the team-specific business objectives are provided to the team by leadership as part of the context, nothing is said about how to actually solve the problems they are assigned. That's where the team has the autonomy and flexibility.

21

Profile: Lea Hickman of Adobe

F or startups or smaller companies, often all it takes is a strong product team with a strong product-oriented CEO or product manager. But, in larger companies, it usually takes more than that. It takes strong *product leadership*, in the very best sense of the word, including providing a compelling product vision and strategy.

One of the absolute hardest assignments in our industry is to try to cause dramatic change in a large and financially successful company. It's easier in many ways if the company is in serious trouble, and it is feeling big pain, because that pain can be used to motivate the change.

Of course, great companies want to disrupt themselves before others disrupt them. The difference between Amazon, Netflix, Google, Facebook, and the legions of large but slowly dying companies is usually exactly that: product leadership.

In 2011, Lea Hickman led product for Adobe's Creative Suite. Lea had spent several years at Adobe helping them to build a very large and successful business for itself—on the order of $2 billion in annual license revenue—with its desktop-based Creative Suite.

One of the absolute hardest assignments in our industry is to try to cause dramatic change in a large and financially successful company.

But Lea knew the market was changing, and the company needed to move from the old desktop-centric, annual-upgrade model, to a subscription-based model supporting all the devices designers were now using—including tablets and mobile in all their many form factors.

More generally, Lea knew that the upgrade model was pushing the company to take the product in directions that were not good for Adobe customers and not good in the long term for Adobe. But change of this magnitude—revenue from Creative Suite was roughly half of Adobe's overall $4 billion in annual revenue—is brutally hard.

Realize that every bone and muscle in the corporate body works to protect that revenue, and so a transition of this magnitude means pushing the company far outside it's comfort zone. Finance, legal, marketing, sales, technology—few in the company would be left untouched.

You can start with the typical concerns:

The finance staff was very worried about the revenue consequences of moving from a license model to a subscription model.

The engineering teams were worried about moving from a two-year release train model to continuous development and deployment, especially while assuring quality. They were also concerned that responsibility for service availability was now going to be much higher.

The sales side expected that this transition would change the way the Creative Suite products were sold. Rather than a large reseller channel, Adobe would now have a direct relationship with their customers. While many people at Adobe generally looked forward to this change, the sales organization knew that this was risky because if things didn't work out well, the channels would probably not be forgiving.

And don't underestimate the emotional changes—to both customers and sales staff—of moving from owning software to renting access to software.

With more than a million customers of the existing Creative Suite, Lea understood the technology adoption curve and that a segment of the customer base would strongly resist a change of this magnitude. Lea understood that it's not just about whether the new Creative Cloud would be *better*, it would also be *different* in some meaningful ways. Some people would need more time to digest this change than others.

Realize also that the Creative Suite is, as the name implies, a *suite* of integration applications—15 major ones and many smaller utilities. So, this meant that not just one product had to transform, but the full suite needed to transform, which dramatically increased the risk and complexity. It is any wonder that few companies are willing to tackle a product transformation of this magnitude?

Lea knew she had a tough job in front of her and her teams. She realized that, for all of these interrelated pieces to be able to move together in parallel, she needed to articulate clearly a compelling vision of the new whole as greater than the sum of the parts.

Lea worked with Adobe's then-CTO, Kevin Lynch, to put together some compelling prototypes showing the power of this new foundation and used this to rally executives and product teams.

Lea then began a sustained and exhausting campaign to communicate continuously with leaders and stakeholders across the entire company. To Lea, there was no such thing as over-communication. A continuous stream of prototypes helped keep people excited about what this new future would bring.

Because of the tremendous success of the Creative Cloud—as of this writing, Adobe generated more than $1 billion in recurring revenue faster than anyone else has—Adobe discontinued new releases of the desktop-based Creative Suite to focus their innovation on the new foundation. Today, more than 9 million creative professionals subscribe to, and depend on, the Creative Cloud. Thanks, in large part to this transition, Adobe has more than *tripled* the market cap it had before the transition. The company today is worth roughly $60 billion.

It's easy to see how big companies with lots of revenue at risk would hesitate to make the changes they need to not only survive but thrive. Lea tackled these concerns and more head-on with a clear and compelling vision and strategy and clear and continuous communication to the many stakeholders.

This is one of the most impressive, nearly superhuman examples I know of a product leader driving massive and meaningful change in a large enterprise company. There's no question in my mind that Adobe would not be where it is today without someone like Lea working tirelessly to drive this change through.

And I'm very happy to say that today Lea is a partner at Silicon Valley Product Group, helping other organizations through the transformation to modern product practices.

III

The Right Product

In Part Two, we considered the people—looking at the structure and roles of strong product teams. In Part Three, we explore how to determine what the product team should be working on.

Product Roadmaps

Overview

Now that we've got some strong product teams, we need to answer this fundamental question: What should our product team work on?

For most companies (especially those described in Chapter 6, "The Root Causes of Failed Product Efforts"), that's not a question the teams have to worry much about because they are usually handed down the things to work on in the form of a product roadmap.

One of the key themes of this book is focusing on *outcome* and not *output*. Realize that typical product roadmaps are all about *output*. Yet, good teams are asked to deliver *business results*.

Most of the product world has the same definition for product roadmap, but there are a few variations. I define *product roadmap* as a *prioritized list of features and projects* your team has been asked to work on. These product roadmaps are usually done on a quarterly basis, but sometimes they are a rolling three months, and some companies do annual roadmaps.

In some cases, product roadmaps come down from management (usually referred to as a *stakeholder-driven roadmap*) and sometimes the roadmap comes from the product manager. They don't usually include little things like bugs and optimizations, but they do normally contain the requested features, projects, and big, multi-team efforts often called *initiatives*. And they typically include due dates or at least time frames for when each item is expected to be delivered.

Management knows that many parts of the company need things from the product organization; yet, we are rarely staffed to be able to do everything that's needed. So, management may help mediate this

battle over the constrained resources. That's where stakeholder-
driven roadmaps are especially
common.

Management has fair reasons
for wanting product roadmaps:

> *Typical roadmaps are the root cause of most waste and failed efforts in product organizations.*

- First, they want to be sure you're working on the highest-value things first.
- Second, they are trying to run a business, which means they need to be able to plan. They want to know when key capabilities will launch so they can coordinate marketing programs, sales force hiring, dependencies with partners, and so on.

These are reasonable desires. Yet, typical roadmaps are the root cause of most waste and failed efforts in product organizations.

Let's explore why product roadmaps are such a problem, and then let's consider the alternatives.

22

The Problems with Product Roadmaps

E ven with the best of intentions, product roadmaps typically lead to very poor business results. I refer to the reasons for this as the two inconvenient truths about product.

The first inconvenient truth is that at least half of our product ideas are just not going to work. There are many reasons for a product idea to not pan out.

Sometimes customers just aren't as excited about this idea as we are, so they choose not to use it or buy it (the *value* isn't there). This is the most common situation.

Sometimes they do want to use it, and they try to use it, but it's so complicated that it's simply more trouble than it's worth, which yields the same result—the users don't use it (the *usability* isn't there).

Sometimes the issue is that the customers might have loved it, but it turns out to be much more involved to build than we first thought, and we simply can't afford the time and cost to deliver (the *feasibility* isn't there).

And, sometimes the issue is that we encounter serious legal, financial, or business constraints that block the solution from launch (the *business viability* isn't there).

If that's not bad enough, the second inconvenient truth is that, even with the ideas that do prove to be valuable, usable, feasible, and viable, it typically takes *several itera-*

> *The issue is that anytime you put a list of ideas on a document entitled "roadmap," no matter how many disclaimers you put on it, people across the company will interpret the items as a commitment.*

tions to get the execution of this idea to the point where it delivers the expected business value that management was hoping for. This is often referred to as *time to money*.

In my experience, there simply is no escaping these inconvenient truths. And I've had the opportunity to work with many truly exceptional product teams. The difference is how product teams deal with these truths.

Weak teams just plod through the roadmap they've been assigned, month after month. And, when something doesn't work—which is often—first they blame it on the stakeholder that requested/demanded the feature and then they try to schedule another iteration on the roadmap, or they suggest a redesign or a different set of features that this time they hope will solve the problem.

If they have enough time and money, they can eventually get there so long as management doesn't run out of patience first (a *big* if).

In contrast, strong product teams understand these truths and embrace them rather than deny them. They are very good at quickly tackling the risks (no matter where that idea originated) and are fast at iterating to an effective solution. This is what product discovery is all about, and it is why I view product discovery as the most important core competency of a product organization.

If we can prototype and test ideas with users, customers, engineers, and business stakeholders in hours and days—rather than in weeks and months—it changes the dynamics, and most important, the results.

It's worth pointing out that it isn't the list of ideas on the roadmap that's the problem. If it was just ideas, there's not much harm in that. The issue is that anytime you put a list of ideas on a document entitled "roadmap," no matter how many disclaimers you put on it, people across the company will interpret the items as a commitment. And that's the crux of the problem, because now you're committed to building and delivering this thing, even when it doesn't solve the underlying problem.

Don't misinterpret this. Sometimes, we do need to commit to a delivery on a date. We try to minimize those cases, but there are always some. But we need to make what is called a *high-integrity commitment*. This will be discussed in detail later, but the key takeaway here is that we need to solve the underlying problem, not just deliver a feature.

23

The Alternative to Roadmaps

In this chapter, I describe the alternative to product roadmaps. It's a big topic, and it touches on issues beyond product roadmaps, such as product culture, morale, empowerment, autonomy, and innovation. But my hope is to lay the foundation here and provide the details in the chapters that follow.

Before we jump into the alternative, however, we need to remind ourselves that roadmaps have existed for so long because they serve two purposes, and these needs don't go away:

- The first purpose is because the management of the company wants to make sure that teams are working on the highest-business-value items first.

- The second purpose is because—since they're trying to run a business—there are cases where they need to make date-based commitments, and the roadmap is where they see and track those commitments (even though in most companies, they rarely trust the dates anymore).

So, to be accepted in most companies, any alternative approach to roadmaps must address these needs at least as well as they are addressed today.

In the empowered product team model this book is predicated on, the teams are themselves equipped to figure out the best ways to solve the particular business problems assigned to them. But for this to happen, it's not enough to have strong people equipped with modern tools and techniques. The product teams need to have the necessary *business context*. They need to have a solid understanding of where the company is heading, and they need to know how their particular team is supposed to contribute to the larger purpose.

For technology companies, there are two main components that provide this business context:

1. **The product vision and strategy.** This describes the big picture of what the organization as a whole is trying to accomplish and what the plan is for achieving that vision. Each of our product teams may have its own areas of focus (for example, buyer teams and seller teams), but it's all supposed to come together to achieve the product vision.

2. **The business objectives**. This describes the specific, prioritized business objectives for each product team.

The idea behind business objectives is simple enough: tell the team what you need them to accomplish and how the results will be measured, and let the team figure out the best way to solve the problems.

Consider this example of a business objective and a measurable, key result. Suppose your product currently requires 30 days for a new customer to onboard. But in order to scale effectively, management believes this needs to be reduced to three hours or less.

That's a good example of a business objective for one or more product teams: "Dramatically reduce the time it takes for a new customer to go live." And one of the measurable key results would be "Average new customer onboarding time less than three hours."

I'll describe much more about product vision and strategy—and business objectives—in the upcoming chapters. But for now I want to emphasize how important it is for each and every product team to know how their work contributes to the larger whole and what the company needs them to focus on right now.

> *It is management's responsibility to provide each product team with the specific business objectives they need to tackle.*

Earlier, I said we needed to acknowledge the two drivers for old-style roadmaps, and the first driver is the desire to work on the highest business value items first.

In the model I'm describing, it is management's responsibility to provide each product team with the specific business objectives they need to tackle. The difference is that they are now prioritizing *business results*, rather than product ideas. And, yes, it is more than a little ironic that we sometimes need to convince management to focus on business results.

The second driver is the occasional need for committing to a hard date. We address this with the concept of *high-integrity commitments*, used for those situations where we need to commit to a date or a specific deliverable.

There are several benefits to this way of working:

- First, the teams are much more motivated when they are free to solve the problem the best way they see fit. It's the missionary versus mercenary thing again. Moreover, the teams are designed to be in the best position to solve these problems.

- Second, the team is not off the hook just by delivering a requested feature or project. The feature must *solve the business problem* (as measured by the key results); otherwise, the team needs to try a different approach to the solution.

- Third, no matter where the idea for the solution comes from, or how smart that person is, very often the initial approach doesn't work out. Rather than pretending this is not the case, this model embraces that likelihood.

It is all about *outcome* rather than output.

There are a few product teams out there that have modified their product roadmaps so that each item is stated as a *business problem to solve* rather than the feature or project that may or may not solve it. These are called *outcome-based roadmaps*.

In general, when I see these, I'm pretty happy because I know the product teams are stepping up to solve business problems rather than build features. Outcome-based roadmaps are essentially equivalent to using a business objective–based system such as the OKR system. It's the format that's different more than the content.

There is a tendency, however, with outcome-based roadmaps to put a deadline date on every item, rather than only on the items with a true date constraint. This practice can have cultural and motivation implications to the team.

High-Integrity Commitments

In most Agile teams, when you even mention the word "commitments" (like knowing what you're going to launch and when it will happen), you get reactions ranging from squirming to denial.

It's a constant struggle between those executives and stakeholders who are trying to run the business (with hiring plans, marketing program spend, partnerships, and contracts depending on specific dates and deliverables) and the product team that is understandably reluctant to commit to dates and deliverables. They're reluctant when they don't yet understand what they need to deliver, and if it will work in terms of delivering the necessary business results, in addition to not knowing how much it will really cost because they don't yet know the solution.

Underlying all of this is the hard-learned lessons of product teams that many of the ideas won't work as we hope and those that could work will typically take several iterations to get to the point where they move the needle enough to be considered a business success.

In a custom software environment, you might just be able to iterate until the business is satisfied with the software (or they just give up on it). In a product company, this won't fly.

Now don't get me wrong—you've just heard how I feel about the perils of conventional roadmaps. Good product companies minimize

(continued)

(continued)

these commitments. But there are always some real commitments that need to be made in order to effectively run a company.

So, what to do?

The key is to understand that the root cause of all this grief about commitments is *when* these commitments are

> *It's a constant struggle between those executives and stakeholders who are trying to run the business and the product team that is understandably reluctant to commit to dates and deliverables.*

made. They are made too early. They are made before we know whether we can deliver on this obligation, and even more important, whether what we deliver will solve the problem for the customer.

In the continuous discovery and delivery model, the discovery work is all about answering these questions before we spend the time and money to build production-quality products.

So, the way we manage commitments is with a little bit of give and take.

We ask the executives and our other stakeholders to give us a little time in product discovery to investigate the necessary solution. We need the time to validate that solution with customers to ensure it has the necessary value and usability, with engineers to ensure its feasibility, and with our stakeholders to ensure it is viable for our business.

Once we have come up with a solution that works for our business, we now can make an informed and high-integrity commitment about when we can deliver and what business results we can expect.

Note that our delivery managers are key to determining any commitment dates. Just because your engineers believe something might take only two weeks to build and deliver, what if that team is already occupied on other work, and they can't start on this work for another month? The delivery managers track these commitments and dependencies.

So, the compromise is straightforward. The product team asks for a little time to do product discovery before commitments are

(continued)

(continued)

made, and then after discovery, we are willing to commit to dates and deliverables so our colleagues can effectively do their jobs as well.

Again, in good companies these types of commitments are minimized, but there are always some. It's important for the organization to get comfortable with making these high-integrity commitments and explain to the company that, while they are not something we do frequently, when we do them, they can depend on the product team delivering on these commitments.

Product Vision

Overview

In this section, I discuss the importance of a compelling and inspiring product vision, and how critical the role of product strategy is in delivering on the product vision.

24

Product Vision and Product Strategy

The Product Vision

The *product vision* describes the future we are trying to create, typically somewhere between two and five years out. For hardware or device-centric companies, it's usually five to 10 years out.

Note that this is not the same as the company mission statement. Examples of mission statements are "organize the world's information" or "make the world more open and connected" or "enable anyone anywhere to buy anything anytime." Mission statements are useful, but they don't say anything about how we plan on accomplishing that. That's what the product vision is for.

Note also that the vision is not in any sense a spec. It's mainly a persuasive piece that might be in the form of a *storyboard*, a narrative such as a white paper, or a special type of prototype referred to as a *visiontype*.

Its primary purpose is to communicate this vision and inspire the teams (and stakeholders, investors, partners—and, in many cases, prospective customers) to want to help make this vision a reality.

When done well, the product vision is one of our most effective recruiting tools, and it serves to motivate the people on your teams to come to work every day. Strong technology people are drawn to an inspiring vision—they want to work on something meaningful.

> *Its primary purpose is to communicate this vision and inspire the teams to want to help make this vision a reality.*

You can do some amount of testing of the vision, but it's not the same as the testing of specific solutions we do in product discovery. In truth, buying into a vision is always a bit of a leap of faith. You likely don't know how, or even if, you'll be able to deliver on the vision. But remember you have several years to discover the solutions. At this stage, you should believe it's a worthwhile pursuit.

The Product Strategy

One of the most basic of all product lessons learned is that trying to please everybody at once will almost certainly please nobody. So, the last thing we should do is embark on a ginormous, multi-year effort to create a release that tries to deliver on the product vision.

The *product strategy* is our sequence of products or releases we plan to deliver on the path to realizing the product vision.

I'm using the phrase "products or releases" here loosely. It might be different versions of the same product, a series of different or related products, or some other set of meaningful milestones.

For most types of businesses, I encourage teams to construct product strategy around a series of product/market fits. There are many variations on this (the strategy for the product strategy, if you will).

For business-focused companies, you might have each product/market fit focus on a different vertical market (e.g., financial services, manufacturing, automotive).

For consumer-focused companies, we often structure each product/market fit around a different customer or user persona. For example, an education-related service might have a strategy that targets high school students first, college students next, and then those already working but who want to learn new skills.

Sometimes, the product strategy is based on geography, where we tackle different regions of the world in an intentional sequence.

And, sometimes, the product strategy is based on achieving a set

> *There's no single approach to product strategy that is ideal for everyone, and you can never know how things might have gone if you sequenced your product work differently. I tell teams that the most important benefit is just that you decided to focus your product work on a single target market at a time.*

of key milestones in some sort of logical and important order. For example, "First deliver critical rating and reviews functionality to developers building e-commerce applications; next, leverage the data generated from this use to create a database of consumer product sentiment; and then leverage these data for advanced product recommendations."

There's no single approach to product strategy that is ideal for everyone, and you can never know how things might have gone if you sequenced your product work differently. I tell teams that the most important benefit is just that you decided to focus your product work on a single target market at a time. So, all teams know we're tackling the manufacturing market now, and that's the type of customers we are obsessing on. Our goal is to come up with the smallest actual deliverable product that makes these manufacturing customers successful. Ideas that come up that pertain to other types of customers or markets are saved for future consideration.

Besides significantly increasing your chance of delivering something that can power your business, the product strategy now gives you a tool to align your product work with your sales and marketing organizations.

We want the sales organization to sell in the markets where we've demonstrated product/market fit. As soon as we demonstrate product/market fit for a new market (usually by developing an initial set of reference customers), we want the sales force to go out and find as many additional customers in that market as possible.

> *The difference between vision and strategy is analogous to the difference between good leadership and good management. Leadership* inspires *and sets the direction, and management helps* get us there.

Let's get back to the concept of providing context to the product teams.

For a product team to be empowered and act with any meaningful degree of autonomy, the team must have a deep understanding of the broader context. This starts with a clear and compelling *product vision*, and the path to achieving that vision is the *product strategy*.

The more product teams you have, the more essential it is to have this unifying vision and strategy for each team to be able to make good choices.

And, just to be clear—the idea is not that every product team has its own product vision. That would miss the point. The idea is that our *organization* has a product vision, and all the product teams in that organization are helping to contribute to making that vision a reality.

Of course, in very large organizations, while the mission statement might apply to the full company, it's likely that each business unit would have its own product vision and strategy.

The difference between vision and strategy is analogous to the difference between good leadership and good management. Leadership *inspires* and sets the direction, and management helps *get us there*.

Most important, the product vision should be *inspiring*, and the product strategy should be *focused*.

Prioritizing Markets

In terms of prioritizing markets, all I said above was to prioritize your markets and focus on them one at a time. I didn't say *how* to prioritize them. There is no one right way to do this, but there are three critical inputs to your decision:

(continued)

(continued)

- The first is market sizing, usually referred to as *total addressable market* (TAM). All things considered equal, we like big markets rather than small markets. But, of course, they're not equal. If the largest market would require two years of product work, yet several of the somewhat smaller but still significant markets are much closer in terms of time to market, most likely everyone in your company from the CEO and head of sales on down would prefer you to deliver on a smaller market sooner.

- The second factor concerns distribution, usually referred to as *go to market* (GTM). Different markets may require different sales channels and go-to-market strategies. Again, even if the market is larger, if that market would require a new sales channel, then most likely we would all prioritize a somewhat smaller market that can leverage our existing sales channels.

- The third factor is a (very rough) estimation of how long it will take, referred to as *time to market* (TTM).

These are typically the three dominant factors for prioritizing your markets, but others can be important also. I typically suggest that the head of product, head of technology, and head of product marketing sit down together to work out your product strategy, balancing these various factors.

25

Principles of Product Vision

These are the 10 key principles for coming up with an effective product vision.

1. **Start with *why*.** This is coincidentally the name of a great book on the value of product vision by Simon Sinek. The central notion here is to use the product vision to articulate your *purpose*. Everything follows from that.

2. **Fall in love with the problem, not with the solution.** I hope you've heard this before, as it's been said many times, in many ways, by many people. But it's very true and something a great many product people struggle with.

3. **Don't be afraid to think big with vision.** Too often I see product visions that are not nearly ambitious enough, the kind of thing we can pull off in six months to a year or so, and not substantial enough to inspire anyone.

4. **Don't be afraid to disrupt yourselves because, if you don't, someone else will.** So many companies focus their efforts on protecting what they have rather than constantly creating new value for their customers.

> *Fall in love with the problem, not with the solution.*

5. **The product vision needs to inspire.** Remember that we need product teams of missionaries, not mercenaries. More than anything else, it is the product vision that will inspire missionary-like passion in the organization. Create something you can get excited about. You can make any product vision meaningful if you focus on how you genuinely help your users and customers.

6. **Determine and embrace relevant and meaningful trends.** Too many companies ignore important trends for far too long. It is not very hard to identify the important trends. What's hard is to help the organization understand how those trends can be leveraged by your products to solve customer problems in new and better ways.

7. **Skate to where the puck is heading, not to where it was.** An important element to product vision is identifying the things that are changing—as well as the things that likely won't be changing—in the time frame of the product vision. Some product visions are wildly optimistic and unrealistic about how fast things will change, and others are far too conservative. This is usually the most difficult aspect of a good product vision.

8. **Be stubborn on vision but flexible on the details.** This Jeff Bezos line is very important. So many teams give up on their product vision far too soon. This is usually called a *vision pivot*, but mostly it's a sign of a weak product organization. It is never easy, so prepare yourself for that. But, also be careful you don't get attached to details. It is very possible that you may have to adjust course to reach your desired destination. That's called a *discovery pivot*, and there's nothing wrong with that.

9. **Realize that any product vision is a leap of faith.** If you could truly validate a vision, then your vision prob-

> *Be stubborn on vision but flexible on the details.*

ably isn't ambitious enough. It will take several years to know. So, make sure what you're working on is meaningful, and recruit people to the product teams who also feel passionate about this problem and then be willing to work for several years to realize the vision.

10. **Evangelize continuously and relentlessly.** There is no such thing as over-communicating when it comes to explaining and selling the vision. Especially in larger organizations, there is simply no escaping the need for near-constant evangelization. You'll find that people in all corners of the company will at random times get nervous or scared about something they see or hear. Quickly reassure them before their fear infects others.

26

Principles of Product Strategy

As we discussed previously, there are any number of approaches to product strategy, but *good* strategies have these five principles in common:

1. **Focus on one target market or persona at a time.** Don't try to please everyone in a single release. Focus on one new target market, or one new target persona, for each release. You'll find that the product will still likely be useful to others, but at least it will be loved by some, and that's key.

2. **Product strategy needs to be aligned with business strategy.** The vision is meant to inspire the organization, but the organization ultimately is there to come up with solutions that deliver on the business strategy. So, for example, if that business strategy involves a change in monetization strategy or business model, then the product strategy needs to be aligned with this.

3. **Product strategy needs to be aligned with sales and go-to-market strategy.** Similarly, if we have a new sales and

> *Obsess over customers, not over competitors.*

marketing channel, we need to ensure that our product strategy is aligned with that new channel. A new sales channel or go-to-market strategy can have far-reaching impact on a product.

4. **Obsess over customers, not over competitors.** Too many companies completely forget about their product strategy once they encounter a serious competitor. They panic and then find themselves chasing their competitor's actions and no longer focusing on their customers. We can't ignore the market, but remember that customers rarely leave us for our competitors. They leave us because we stop taking care of them.

5. **Communicate the strategy across the organization.** This is part of evangelizing the vision. It's important that all key business partners in the company know the customers we're focused on now and which are planned for later. Stay especially closely synced with sales, marketing, finance, and service.

CHAPTER
27

Product Principles

I always like to complement the product vision and product strategy with a set of product principles.

Where the product vision describes the future you want to create, and the product strategy describes your path to achieving that vision, the product principles speak to the *nature of the products you want to create*.

Product principles are not a list of features, and they are not tied to any one product release. The principles are aligned with the product vision for an entire product line.

A good set of principles may inspire some product features, but it's more about what the company and product teams believe is important.

As an example, early on at eBay we found we needed a product principle that spoke to the relationship between buyers and sellers. Most of the revenue came from sellers, so we had a strong incentive to find ways to please sellers, but we soon realized that the real reason sellers loved us was because we provided them with buyers. This realization led to a critical principle that stated, "In cases where the needs of the buyers and the sellers conflict, we will prioritize the needs of the buyer, because that's actually the most important thing we can do for sellers."

These are what principles are all about. You can imagine how this type of principle would help with designing and building a marketplace and how many issues could be resolved by simply keeping it in mind.

Whether you choose to go public with your principles depends

Where the product vision describes the future you want to create, and the product strategy describes your path to achieving that vision, the product principles speak to the nature of the products you want to create.

on your purpose. In many cases, the principles are simply a tool for the product teams. But, in other cases, the principles serve as a clear statement of what you believe—intended for your users, customers, partners, suppliers, investors, and your employees.

Product Objectives

Overview

I was extremely fortunate to have started my career at HP as an engineer during their heyday, when they were known as the industry's most successful and enduring example of consistent innovation and execution.

As part of HP's internal engineering management training program called *The HP Way*, I was introduced to a business objective–based system known as MBO—*management by objectives*.

Dave Packard claimed: "No [tool] has contributed more to Hewlett-Packard's success. [MBO] is the antithesis of management by control."

The MBO system was refined and improved at several companies over the years, most notably by the legendary Andy Grove at Intel. Today, the primary business objective management system we use is known as the OKR system—*objectives and key results*.

John Doerr brought the technique from Intel to a very young Google, and a couple decades after Dave Packard attributed much of HP's success to MBO, Larry Page said essentially the same thing about the importance of the OKR process on Google's success.

The concept is straightforward and based on two fundamental principles:

1. The first can easily be summed up with the famous General George Patton quote I mentioned earlier: "Never tell people how to do things. Tell them what to do, and they will surprise you with their ingenuity."

2. The second was captured by HP's tagline of that era: "When performance is measured by results." The idea here is that you can release all the features you want, but if it doesn't solve the underlying business problem, you haven't really solved anything.

The first principle is fundamentally about how to empower and motivate people to get them to do their best work, and the second is about how to meaningfully measure progress.

So much has changed in our industry over the years, but these two fundamental management principles are still at the foundation of how the best tech companies and teams operate.

While there are several work-able systems and tools for managing these business objectives, in this book, I'll focus on the OKR system technique. Most of the major successful tech companies have been using it for several years now. It seems to have hit some sort of tipping point and is now spreading globally.

> *The first principle is fundamentally about how to empower and motivate people to get them to do their best work, and the second is about how to meaningfully measure progress.*

While the concept of team objectives might sound straightforward, there are many ways to institutionalize this across product teams and organizations, and it can take a few quarters before the organization finds its groove.

CHAPTER
28

The OKR Technique

The Objectives and Key Results (OKR) technique is a tool for management, focus, and alignment. As with any tool, there are many ways to use it. Here are the critical points for you to keep in mind when using the tool for product teams in product organizations.

1. Objectives should be qualitative; key results need to be quantitative/measurable.

2. Key results should be a measure of *business* results, not output or tasks.

3. The rest of the company will use OKRs a bit differently, but for the product management, design, and technology organization, focus on the *organization's* objectives and the objectives for each *product team*, which are designed to roll up and achieve the organization's objectives. Don't let personal objectives or functional team objectives dilute or confuse the focus.

4. Find a good cadence for your organization (typically, annually for an organization's objectives and quarterly for a team's objectives).

> *Key results should be a measure of business results, not output or tasks.*

5. Keep the number of objectives and key results for the organization and for each team small (one to three objectives, with one to three key results each is typical).

6. It's critical that every product team *track their active progress* against their objectives (which is typically weekly).

7. The objectives do not need to cover every little thing the team does, but they should cover what the team *needs to accomplish*.

8. It's important that, one way or another, teams feel accountable to achieving their objectives. If they fail substantially, it's worth having a post-mortem/retrospective with some of their peers or management.

9. Agree as an organization on how you will be evaluating or scoring your key results. There are different approaches to this, and it's in large part a reflection of your particular company culture. What's important here is consistency across the organization, so that teams know when they can depend on one another. It's common to define a score of 0 (on a scale from 0 to 1.0) if you essentially make no progress, 0.3 if you just did the bare minimum—what you know you can achieve, 0.7 if you've accomplished more than the minimum and have really done what you'd hoped you would achieve, and 1.0 if you've really surprised yourselves and others with a truly exceptional result, beyond what people were even hoping for.

10. Establish very clear and consistent ways to indicate when a key result is in reality a *high-integrity commitment* (described earlier) rather than a normal objective. In other words, for most key results, you may be shooting for that 0.7 score. But for a high-integrity commitment, these are special, and it's more binary. You either delivered what you promised or you didn't.

11. Be very transparent (across the product and technology organization) on what objectives each product team is working on and their current progress.

12. Senior management (CEO and executive team) is responsible for the organization's objectives and key results. The heads of product and technology are responsible for the product team objectives (and ensuring they deliver on the organization's objectives). The individual product teams are responsible for proposing the key results for each objective they've been assigned. It is normal to have a give-and-take process each quarter as the OKRs are finalized for each team and for the organization.

29

Product Team Objectives

The OKR technique has enjoyed considerable success, especially inside technology product organizations, from large to small. And there have been some very important lessons learned as teams and organizations work to improve their ability to execute.

OKRs are a very general tool that can be used by anyone in the organization, in any role, or even for your use in your personal life. However, as with any tool, some ways of applying them are better than others.

Throughout this book, I emphasize the importance of a product team. Recall that a product team is a *cross-functional* set of professionals, typically comprised of a product manager, a product designer, and a small number of engineers. In addition, there are sometimes additional people with specialized skills included on the team, such as a data analyst, a user researcher, or a test automation engineer.

Also recall that each product team typically is responsible for some significant part of the company's product offering or technology. For example, one product team might be responsible for mobile apps for drivers, another for mobile apps for riders, another might be responsible for secure payment handling, and so on.

The key is that these people with their different skill sets usually come from different functional departments in the company, but they sit and work all day—every day—with their cross-functional team to solve hard business and technology problems.

It's not unusual in larger organizations to have on the order of 20 to 50 of these cross-functional product teams, each responsible for different areas, and each product team with its own objectives to work on.

For companies using the OKR system, the problems these teams are asked to tackle are, as you might expect, communicated and tracked through the product team's OKRs. The OKRs also help to ensure that each team is aligned with the objectives of the company.

Moreover, as an organization scales, OKRs become an increasingly necessary tool for ensuring that each product team understands how they are contributing to the greater whole, coordinating work across teams, and avoiding duplicate work.

The reason this is so important to understand is that when organizations first start with OKRs, there's a common tendency to have each *functional* department create their own OKRs for their own organization. For example, the design department might have objectives related to moving to a responsive design; the engineering department might have objectives related to improving the scalability and performance of the architecture; and the quality department might have objectives relating to the test and release automation.

The problem is that the individual members of each of these functional departments are the actual members of a cross-functional product team. The product team has business-related objectives (for example, to reduce the customer acquisition cost, to increase the number of daily active users, or to reduce the time to onboard a new customer), but each person on the team may have their own set of objectives that cascade down through their functional manager.

Imagine if the engineers were told to spend their time on re-platforming, the designers on moving to a responsive design, and QA on retooling. While each of these may be worthy activities, the chances of solving the business problems that the cross-functional teams were created to solve are not high.

What all too often happens in this case is that the people on the product teams are conflicted as to where they should be spending their time. This results in confusion, frustration, and disappointing

> *If you deploy OKRs for your product organization, the key is to focus your OKRs at the product team level.*

results from leadership and individual contributors alike.

But this is easily avoided.

If you deploy OKRs for your product organization, the key is to focus your OKRs at the *product team level*.

This means don't let functional team or individual person OKRs confuse the issue.

Focus the attention of the individuals on their product team objectives. If different functional organizations (such as design, engineering, or quality assurance) have larger objectives (such as responsive design, technical debt, and test automation), they should be discussed and prioritized at the leadership team level along with the other business objectives, and then incorporated into the relevant product team's objectives.

Note that it's not a problem for managers of the functional areas to have individual objectives relating to their organization. This is because these people aren't conflicted, as they're not normally serving on a product team.

For example, the head of UX design might be responsible for a strategy for migrating to a responsive design; the head of engineering might be responsible for delivering a strategy around managing technical debt; the head of product management might be responsible for delivering a product vision; or the head of QA might be responsible for selecting a test automation tool.

It's also not normally a big problem if individual contributors (such as a particular engineer, designer, or product manager) has a small number of personal growth-related objectives (such as improving their knowledge of a particular technology). This assumes the individual isn't committing to a burden that will interfere with their ability to contribute their part to their product team, which of course is their primary responsibility.

The key is that the cascading of OKRs in a product organization needs to be up from the cross-functional product teams to the company or business-unit level.

Product @ Scale

Overview

We have thus far discussed product vision, strategy, and business objectives. In truth, as an early stage startup, you can survive without any of these for a while. It's amazing how far you can get by focusing on meeting the needs of some early customers.

However, the need for this vision and business-objective context becomes truly serious at scale.

Keeping a small number of teams and their engineers doing useful stuff is not very hard, but getting good results out of a medium—or, especially, large—organization can be truly challenging.

Realize also that by the time the company has scaled, the original co-founders may have moved on, so there may very well be a void. Teams need this context. It is nearly impossible for them to make good decisions and do good work without it.

The main ways these issues show up is diminished morale, lack of innovation, and reduced velocity.

30

Product Objectives @ Scale

The OKR system is very scalable. I would argue some sort of tool for managing and aligning work is critical to scaling effectively, but it's also true that many companies do struggle with scaling their use of OKRs.

In this chapter, I shine a light on what needs to change as you use the OKR system at scale. Remember that I'm just talking about the product and technology organization here (product management, user experience design, and engineering), and while you can use the techniques I'm about to describe at any scale, I am focused here on growth stage or enterprise organizations.

1. With startups or small organizations, when everyone essentially knows what everyone else is doing and why, it's normal for each product team to propose their objectives and key results. There's some amount of give and take, and then people get to work. With larger organizations, product teams need more help.

The first help they need is a very clear understanding of the organization-level objectives. Let's say that the top two objectives for the company are to improve customer lifetime value and expand globally. Let's also say you have on the order of 25 product teams. All the product teams likely have thoughts on both of these organizational objectives, but, clearly, the company will need to be smart about which teams pursue each objective. Some teams might focus on only one, others might contribute to both, and yet other teams may be tackling critical work beyond those two objectives.

Leadership (especially the head of product, head of technology, and head of design) will need to discuss the company objectives and which teams are best suited to pursue each objective.

2. Moreover, at scale, it is very common to have some significant number of product teams that are there in support of the other product teams. These are often called *platform product teams*, or *shared services product teams*. They are very high leverage, but they are a little different in that they generally don't directly serve customers. They serve customers indirectly, usually through the higher-level, solution-focused product teams. These platform teams will get requests from most or even all the higher-level product teams, and they are there to help them succeed. But, again, leadership will need to help coordinate the objectives for these teams and make sure we coordinate the dependencies and align the interests.

3. Once you have your objectives, there is a very critical reconciliation process in which the leadership team looks at the proposed key results from the product teams and identifies gaps and then looks to what might be adjusted to cover those gaps (for example, enlisting the help of additional teams or reviewing the priority of the work).

4. At scale, it's much harder to know what product teams are working on which objectives and the progress they are making. There are now a variety of online tools that help organizations make the objectives transparent to the organization. But even with these tools, we lean on management to help connect the dots between teams.

5. The larger the organization, the longer the list of high-integrity commitments that are needed, and the more actively they need to be managed and tracked. Delivery managers play a key role in tracking and managing these dependencies and our commitments.

6. In many enterprise scale organizations, there are essentially multiple business units, and in this case, we would expect that there are corporate level OKRs, but there would also be business unit–level OKRs, and the product teams would roll up into those.

> *When using OKRs at scale, there's a larger burden on leadership and management to ensure that the organization is truly aligned, that each and every product team understands how they fit into the mix, and that they are there to contribute.*

In summary, when using OKRs at scale, there's a larger burden on leadership and management to ensure that the organization is truly aligned, that each and every product team understands how they fit into the mix, and what they are there to contribute.

31

Product Evangelism

Product evangelism is, as Guy Kawasaki put it years ago, "selling the dream." It's helping people imagine the future and inspiring them to help create that future.

If you're a startup founder, a CEO, or a head of product, this is a very big part of your job, and you'll have a hard time assembling a strong team if you don't get good at it.

If you're a product manager—especially at a large company—and you're not good at evangelism, there's a very strong chance that your product efforts will get derailed before they see the light of day. And even if product does manage to ship, it will likely go the way of thousands of other large company efforts and wither on the vine.

We've talked about how important it is to have a team of missionaries, not mercenaries, and evangelism is a key responsibility to make this happen. The responsibility for this falls primarily on the product manager.

There are several techniques to help communicate the value of what you're proposing to your team, colleagues, stakeholders, executives, and investors. Here are my top-10 pieces of advice for product managers to sell the dream:

1. **Use a prototype.** For many people, it's way too hard to see the forest through the trees. When all you have is a bunch of user stories, it can be difficult to see the big picture and how things hang together (or even *if* they hang together). A prototype lets them clearly see the forest *and* the trees.

2. **Share the pain.** Show the team the customer pain you are addressing. This is why I love to bring engineers along for customer visits and meetings. For many people, they have to see (or experience) the pain themselves to get it.

3. **Share the vision.** Make sure you have a very clear understanding of your product vision, product strategy, and product principles. Show how your work contributes to this vision and is true to the principles.

4. **Share learnings generously.** After every user test or customer visit, share your learnings—not just the things that went well, but share the problems, too. Give your team the information they need to help come up with the solution.

5. **Share credit generously.** Make sure the team views it as *their* product, not just *your* product. However, when things don't go well, step forward and take responsibility for the miss and show the team you're learning from the mistakes as well. They'll respect you for it.

6. **Learn how to give a great demo.** This is an especially important skill to use with customers and key execs. We're not trying to teach them how to operate the product, and we're not trying to do a user test on them. We're trying to show them the value of what we're building. A demo is not training, and it's not a test. It's a persuasive tool. Get really, really good at it.

7. **Do your homework.** Your team and your stakeholders will all be much more likely to follow you if they believe you know what you're talking about. Be the undisputed expert on your users and customers. And be the undisputed expert on your market, including your competitors and the relevant trends.

8. **Be genuinely excited.** If you're not excited about your product, you should probably fix that—either by changing what you work on or by changing your role.

> *Absolutely be sincere, but let people see you're genuinely excited. Enthusiasm really is contagious.*

9. **Learn to show some enthusiasm.** Assuming you're genuinely excited, it's amazing to me how many product managers are so bad or so uncomfortable at showing enthusiasm. This matters—a *lot*. Absolutely be sincere, but let people see you're genuinely excited. Enthusiasm really is contagious.

10. **Spend time with your team.** If you're not spending significant face time with your designer and every engineer on your team, then they can't see the enthusiasm in your eyes. If your team is not co-located, you'll need to make a special effort to travel there and do this at least every couple months. Spending some personal time with every last person on the team pays off big in their level of motivation and, as a result, in the velocity of the team. It's worth your time.

If your company is midsize to large, then it's normal to have product marketing play the role of evangelist with your customers and your sales force. You still may be called on to help out on the big deals and partnerships, but you'll need to focus your evangelism on your team because the best thing you can do for your customers is to provide them with a great product.

32

Profile: Alex Pressland of the BBC

I have to admit I have a soft spot for the BBC. They've been around for nearly 100 years, but they embraced technology and the Internet relatively early. I've seen so many amazing product people come out of the BBC, and many are now spread across Europe and beyond.

Back in 2003—a full four years before the debut of the iPhone—a young product manager at the BBC, Alex Pressland, had just finished leading a product effort that enabled the BBC to be one of the first media companies in the world to syndicate content. Most people at the BBC had no idea why this was important or even desirable, but Alex understood that this enabling technology could be used in new and unanticipated ways to increase the BBC's reach, a major part of the institution's mission.

Because Alex understood the potential for IP-based syndicated content technology, she started searching for new and useful ways to put this technology to use. She began by looking at people in the United Kingdom who were not being reached by the BBC's conventional broadcast media (TVs and radios in homes and cars).

One early use she identified was large electronic billboard screens in many city center venues that were capable of displaying video. But she observed that these venues were just playing the same thing you could watch on your television at home, even though the context and audience was very different.

So, Alex proposed a series of experiments in which she would have editorial teams assemble specific tailored content suitable for specific venues and audiences, and then she would measure the audience reach and engagement.

While this might sound obvious today, at the time this was a very foreign concept to the BBC's *broadcast* journalism culture. There was a long list of obstacles in trying to push the BBC in this direction, not the least of which was editorial and legal.

Editorial wasn't used to the model in which content would be created and then delivered in different contexts. This gets to the heart of the BBC editorial culture and required considerable persuasion to show why this was a very good thing for both the BBC and for the audience.

Legal wasn't used to distribution via IP-enabled devices. Imagine the stack of content-licensing agreements that would need to be updated or renegotiated.

The results of Alex's experiments and early successes, however, gave her the confidence to propose to BBC leadership a new product vision and strategy which she called "BBC Out of Home."

It's important to note that she did this as an *individual contributor* product manager.

This work ended up fueling a dramatic shift at the BBC—from broadcast content to content distribution—and this work dramatically affected reach and soon became the basis for BBC's mobile efforts. Today, more than 50 million people around the world depend on BBC's mobile offerings every week.

> *With large enterprise companies, it's never easy to drive substantial change, but this is exactly what strong product managers figure out how to do.*

This is not just a story about applying technology to solve problems; it's also a story about the power of force of will. With large enterprise companies, it's never easy to drive substantial change, but this is exactly what strong product managers figure out how to do.

Alex went on from the BBC to have a terrific career at several tech and media companies and now is a product leader in New York.

PART

IV

The Right Process

We've explored product teams in Part Two, and we described how to decide what each team needs to focus on in Part Three. In Part Four, I explain how product teams do their job. We'll work through the techniques, activities, and best practices used to repeatedly discover and deliver successful products.

Even though this part is titled "The Right Process," I hope you'll soon realize that the right process is not any *single* process. Rather, it's more accurately described as a combination of techniques, mindset, and culture.

I mostly emphasize discovery techniques, as our focus is on product managers, and that is their primary responsibility.

The bulk of the product manager's time needs to be focused on working with her product team, with her key stakeholders, and with her customers to discover solutions that her customers love and that work for the business.

Keep in mind, however, that the product manager and product designer do need to ensure that they're available to answer questions from the engineers that arise during delivery activities. Normally, answering these delivery questions is on the order of half an hour to an hour of time per day.

Product Discovery

Overview

Most of us are working on solving some pretty hard problems, and it usually ends up taking some fairly complex systems to power these solutions. For most teams, there are two very significant challenges to tackle.

First, discovering in detail what the customer solution needs to be. That includes everything from making sure there are enough customers that even need this solution (the demand) and then coming up with a solution that works for our customers and for our business.

Even harder, we need to make sure we come up with a *single solution* that works for *many* customers, and not a series of *specials*. To do this, we need to be able to test out many ideas, and we need to do this quickly and inexpensively.

Second, we need to ensure we deliver a robust and scalable implementation that our customers can depend on for consistently reliable value. Your team needs to be able to *release with confidence*. While you'll never have 100 percent confidence, you should not have to release and pray.

So, we need to learn fast, yet also release with confidence.

It's understandable that many people might naturally view these two difficult goals as at odds with each other. We are in a big hurry to push something out to learn what works and what doesn't. Yet, we don't want to release something that's not ready for prime time and risk hurting our customers and damaging our brand.

I spend a lot of my time visiting with product teams. I have on occasion been called out for pushing hard one minute for the team to be much more aggressive in getting out to customers and getting early feedback on their ideas, and then just minutes later pushing that

> *We need to learn fast, yet also release with confidence.*

same team hard not to compromise their standards on releasing scalable, fault-tolerant, reliable, high-performance, secure software.

You might also recognize this problem in another guise. Many teams get into a lot of grief with the concept of a minimum viable product (MVP) because on the one hand we are very motivated to get this out in front of customers fast to get feedback and learn. And, on the other hand, when we do get out there fast, people feel like this so-called product is an embarrassment to the brand and the company. How could we possibly consider launching this?

In this section, I clarify how strong teams work to meet these dual and simultaneous objectives of rapid learning in discovery, yet building stable and solid releases in delivery.

In general, I find that most product teams have a much better sense of how to accomplish the second goal of delivering solid software than how to accomplish the first goal of rapid experimentation and discovery. Continuous delivery is a good example of an advanced delivery technique I find in teams that understand the importance of a series of small, incremental changes to a complex system.

Part of what causes confusion is a dilution of what is really meant when we call something a "product" or "product-quality" or "productized" or "live in production."

I always try hard to reserve the term *product* to describe the state at which we can run a business on it. Specifically, it is scalable and performant to the degree necessary. It has a strong suite of automated regression tests. It is instrumented to collect the necessary analytics. It has been internationalized and localized where appropriate. It is maintainable. It is consistent with the brand promise. And, most important, it is something the team can release with confidence.

This is not easy—it's where most of the time goes when our engineers are building. As such, we try very hard not to waste this effort.

Doing all this work when the product manager isn't even sure this is the solution the customer wants or needs is a recipe for product failure and big waste. So, the purpose of product discovery is to make sure we have some evidence that when we ask the engineers to build a production-quality product, it won't be a wasted effort. And, this is why we have so many different techniques in product discovery.

We've got techniques for getting a much deeper understanding of our users and customers, and for validating product ideas both qualitatively and quantitatively. And, in fact, most of the techniques don't require the developer's time (which is important, because we appreciate how much time and effort needs to go into creating production-quality software in delivery).

Much of the key to effective product discovery is getting access to our customers without trying to push our quick experiments into production.

If you are an early stage startup and you have no customers, then of course this is not really an issue (and it's very likely premature to even be creating production-quality software).

But, for most of us, we have real customers and real revenue, so we do have to care about this. Later in this section, we'll talk about the techniques that allow for rapid experimentation in a responsible way in larger, enterprise companies.

But here's the key. If you want to *discover* great products, it really is essential that you get your ideas in front of real users and customers early and often.

If you want to *deliver* great products, you want to use best practices for engineering and try not to override the engineers' concerns.

33

Principles of Product Discovery

The *purpose* of product discovery is to address these critical risks:

- Will the customer buy this, or choose to use it? (*Value risk*)
- Can the user figure out how to use it? (*Usability risk*)
- Can we build it? (*Feasibility risk*)
- Does this solution work for our business? (*Business viability risk*)

And it's not enough that it's just the product manager's opinion on these questions. We need to collect *evidence*.

When it comes to *how* we do product discovery, there are a set of core principles that drive how we work. If you understand these, you will understand not only how to work well today but also how to easily incorporate new techniques as they emerge in the future.

1. We know we can't count on our customers (or our executives or stakeholders) to tell us what to build.

   > *Customers don't know what's possible, and with technology products, none of us know what we really want until we actually see it.*

   Customers don't know what's possible, and with technology products, none of us know what we really want until we actually see it. It's not that customers or our executives are necessarily wrong; it's just that it's our job to make sure the solution we deliver solves the underlying problem. This is probably the most fundamental principle in all of modern product. Historically, in the vast majority of innovations in our industry, the customers had no idea that what they now love was even a possibility. This is only becoming truer with time.

2. The most important thing is to establish compelling value.

   It's all hard, but the hardest part of all is creating the necessary *value* so that customers ultimately *choose* to buy or to use. We can survive for a while with usability issues or performance issues, but without the core value, we really have nothing. As a result, this is generally where we'll need to spend most of our discovery time.

3. As hard and important as the engineering is, coming up with a good user experience is usually even harder, and more critical to success.

   While every product team has engineers, not every team has the necessary product design skills, and even when they do, are they being used the way we need to use them?

4. Functionality, design, and technology are inherently intertwined.

   In the old waterfall model, the market drove the functionality (aka the *requirements*), which drove the design, which drove the implementation.

   Today, we know that the technology drives (and enables) the functionality as much as the other way around. We know that technology drives (and enables) design. We know that design drives (and enables) functionality. You don't have to look further than your own phone to see numerous examples of both. The point is that all three of these are completely intertwined. This is the single biggest reason we push so hard for the product manager, product designer, and tech lead to sit physically adjacent to each other.

5. We expect that many of our ideas won't work out, and the ones that do will require several iterations.

> *"The most important thing is to know what you can't know."*

To quote Marc Andreessen, "The most important thing is to know what you can't know," and we can't know in advance which of our ideas will work with customers and which won't. So, we approach discovery with the mindset that many, if not most, of our ideas won't work out. The most common reason for this is value, but sometimes the design is too complicated, and sometimes it would take far too long to build, and sometimes there turn out to be legal or privacy issues. The point is we need to be open to solving the underlying problem in different ways if necessary.

6. We must validate our ideas on real users and customers.

One of the most common traps in product is to believe that we can anticipate our customer's actual response to our products. We might be basing that on actual customer research or on our own experiences, but in any case, we know today that we must validate our actual ideas on real users and customers. We need to do this before we spend the time and expense to build an actual product, and not after.

7. Our goal in discovery is to validate our ideas the fastest, cheapest way possible.

Discovery is about the need for speed. This lets us try out many ideas, and for the promising ideas, try out multiple approaches. There are many different types of ideas, many different types of products, and a variety of different risks that we need to address (value risk, usability risk, feasibility risk, and business risk). So, we have a wide range of techniques, each suitable to different situations.

8. We need to validate the feasibility of our ideas during discovery, not after.

   If the first time your developers see an idea is at sprint planning, you have failed. We need to ensure the feasibility before we decide to build, not after. Not only does this end up saving a lot of wasted time, but it turns out that getting the engineer's perspective earlier also tends to improve the solution itself, and it's critical for shared learning.

9. We need to validate the business viability of our ideas during discovery, not after.

   Similarly, it is absolutely critical to ensure that the solution we build will meet the needs of our business—*before* we take the time and expense to build out that product. Business viability includes financial considerations, marketing (both brand and go-to-market considerations), sales, legal, business development, and senior executives. Few things destroy morale or confidence in the product manager more than finding out after a product has been built that the product manager did not understand some essential aspect of the business.

10. It's about shared learning.

    One of the keys to having a team of missionaries rather than a team of mercenaries is that the team has learned together. They have seen the customer's pain together, they have watched together as some ideas failed and others worked, and they all understand the context for why this is important and what needs to be done.

    Everything that follows is based on these core principles.

Ethics: Should We Build It?

In general, product discovery is about tackling risks around *value*, *usability*, *feasibility*, and *business viability*. However, in some cases, there's an additional risk: *ethics*.

I know this is a sensitive topic, and I don't want to sound like I'm preaching or condescending in the least, but I personally

(continued)

(continued)

encourage the teams I work with to also consider the question, "*Should* we build it?"

> *I encourage product teams to consider the ethical implications of their solutions, too.*

You may think this is a matter of doing something illegal, but in the vast majority of cases where ethics is an issue, it's not usually a matter of law. Rather, just because we have the technology to build something, and even if it otherwise works to accomplish the specific business objective, this does not necessarily mean that we *should* build it.

More commonly, the issue is that our technology and design skills are such that we might come up with a solution that meets our business objectives (for example, around engagement, growth, or monetization) but can end up with a side effect of causing harm to users or the environment.

So, I encourage product teams to consider the ethical implications of their solutions, too. When a significant ethical risk is identified, see if you can't find alternative solutions that solve the problem in a way that doesn't have negative consequences.

I have one final, but critically important, note about raising ethics issues with senior management. You absolutely need to have a strong understanding of your business, especially how you make money. You need to use good judgment and be sensitive in your discussion. You are not there to try to police the organization but, rather, to identify issues and bring potential solutions.

Discovery Iterations

Most product teams normally think of an *iteration* as a delivery activity. If you release weekly, you think in terms of one-week iterations.

(continued)

(continued)

But we also have the concept of an iteration in discovery. We loosely define an *iteration* in discovery as trying out at least one new idea or approach. It's true that ideas come in all shapes and sizes, and some are much riskier than others, but the purpose of discovery is to do this much faster and cheaper than we can do in delivery.

To set your expectations, teams competent in modern discovery techniques can generally test on the order of 10–20 iterations *per week*. This may sound like a lot to you, but you'll soon see that's not so hard at all with modern discovery techniques.

Also, realize that many iterations never make it beyond just you, your designer, and your tech lead. The very act of creating a prototype often exposes problems that cause you to change your mind. As a rule of thumb, an iteration in discovery should be *at least* an order of magnitude less time and effort than an iteration in delivery.

> *To set your expectations, teams competent in modern discovery techniques can generally test on the order of 10–20 iterations* per week.

34

Discovery Techniques Overview

There is no one perfect taxonomy for discovery techniques because several of the techniques are helpful for multiple different situations. Regardless, following are the key techniques in the framework that I personally use and find helpful.

Discovery Framing Techniques

Framing techniques help us to quickly identify the underlying issues that must be tackled during product discovery. If we're handed a potential solution, we need to clarify the underlying problem to be solved. We need to tease out the risks and determine where it makes sense to focus our time. We also need to ensure that we understand how our work fits in with the work of other teams.

Discovery Planning Techniques

There are a few techniques that are useful throughout the product discovery effort and help with identifying the bigger challenges and planning how you'll attack this work. We'll discuss these here.

Discovery Ideation Techniques

There are, of course, any number of ways to come up with ideas. But some sources are better than others in their potential for keeping us focused on the most important problems. Ideation techniques are designed to provide the product team with a wealth of promising solutions aimed at the problems we're focused on now.

Discovery Prototyping Techniques

Our go-to tool for product discovery is typically a prototype. We'll discuss the four main types of prototypes and highlight what each type is best suited for.

Discovery Testing Techniques

Product discovery is mostly about quickly trying out an idea. We are essentially trying to separate the good ideas from the bad. Here we are defining a good idea as one that solves the underlying problem in a way that customers will buy, they can figure out how to use, we have the time and skills and technology on the team to build, and that works for the various aspects of our business.

It's important to recognize that many ideas don't have that much risk associated with them. They may be very straightforward. Or they might just have one area that's a risk, such as our legal department's concern about a potential privacy issue.

Occasionally, however, we need to tackle much tougher problems, and we may in fact have significant risks in most or even all these areas.

So, the way to think about discovery is that we only validate what we need to, and then we pick the right technique based on the particular situation.

Testing Feasibility

These techniques are designed for the engineers to address areas where they identify concerns. The solution being tested might require some piece of technology that the team has no experience with. There may be significant scale or performance challenges. Or there might be third-party components that need to be evaluated.

Testing Usability

These techniques are designed for the product designers to address areas where they have identified concerns. Many of our products have complex workflows and the designers need to ensure their interaction designs make sense to the user and potential sources of confusion are identified and pre-empted.

Testing Value

Much of our time in product discovery is spent validating value or working to increase the perceived value. If it's a new product, we need to ensure that customers will buy it, at the price we need to charge, and that they'll switch from whatever they're using today. If it's an existing product, and we are improving that product (such as with a new feature or a new design), where the customer has already bought the product, we need to ensure the customers will choose to use the new feature or new design.

Testing Business Viability

Sadly, it's not enough to create a product or solution that our customers love, that is usable, and that our engineers can deliver. The product also must work for our business. This is what it means to be *viable*. This means that we can afford the cost of building and provisioning the product and the costs to market and sell the product. It needs to be something our sales force is capable of selling. It means that the solution needs to also work for our business development partners. It needs to work for our legal colleagues. It needs to be consistent with our company's brand promise. These techniques are about validating these types of risks.

Transformation Techniques

When working to migrate your organization from working the way you do today to working the way you believe you need to, there are a set of techniques that have proved to be helpful for transforming how you work.

So, as you can see, we need quite a range of techniques. Some of the techniques are *quantitative*, and some are *qualitative*. Some of the techniques are designed to collect *proof* (or at least statistically significant results), and some are designed to collect *evidence*. All are designed to help us *learn quickly*.

> *I am sharing the techniques here that I believe are essential for any modern product team.*

To be clear, I am sharing the techniques here that I believe are essential for any modern product team. Over the course of a year or two, you will probably use each of the techniques at least several times. There are, as you might imagine, many other useful techniques based on specific types of products or situations, and new techniques are always emerging. But, these are your go-to techniques.

Discovery Framing Techniques

Overview

Much of our product discovery work doesn't require a lot of framing or planning. We need to come up with a solution to a particular problem, and often this is straightforward, and we can proceed directly to delivery work.

But for many efforts, this is decidedly not the case, and some framing and true problem solving becomes critically important. Big projects—and, especially, *initiatives* (projects spanning multiple teams)—are common examples.

In this section, I consider how we frame our discovery work to ensure alignment and to identify key risks.

There are really two goals here:

1. The first is to ensure the team is all on the same page in terms of clarity of purpose and alignment. In particular, we need to agree on the business objective we're focused on, the specific problem we are intending to solve for our customers, which user or customers you're solving that problem for, and how you will know if you've succeeded. These should align directly to your product team's objectives and key results.

2. The second purpose is to identify the big risks that will need to be tackled during the discovery work. I find that most teams tend to gravitate toward a particular type of risk that they are most comfortable with.

Two examples I often find are teams that immediately proceed to tackling technology risks— especially performance or scale— and teams that zero in on usability risks. They know this change

> *Ensure the team is all on the same page in terms of clarity of purpose and alignment.*

involves a complex workflow, and they're nervous about that, so they want to dive in right there.

Those are both legitimate risks, but in my experience, they are generally the easier risks to tackle.

We must also consider *value* risk—do the customers want this particular problem solved and is our proposed solution good enough to get people to switch from what they have now?

And then there's the often-messy business risk, where we have to make sure that the solution we come up with in discovery works for the different parts of our company. Here are some common examples of that:

- Financial risk—can we afford this solution?
- Business development risk—does this solution work for our partners?
- Marketing risk—is this solution consistent with our brand?
- Sales risk—is this solution something our sales staff is equipped to sell?
- Legal risk—is this something we can do from a legal or compliance perspective?
- Ethical risk—is this solution something we should do?

For many things, we won't have concerns along these dimensions, but, when we do, it's something that we must tackle aggressively.

If the product manager, designer, and tech lead do not feel there's a significant risk in any of these areas, then normally we would just proceed to delivery—fully realizing there's a chance the team will occasionally be proved wrong. This, however, is preferable to the alternative of having the team be extremely conservative and test every assumption.

We like to use our discovery time and validation techniques for those situations in which we know there's a significant risk, or where members of the team disagree.

There are many ways to assess an opportunity. Some companies require significant rigor and analysis, and others just leave it to the product team's judgment.

In this section, I describe three of my favorite techniques, each for different-sized efforts:

1. An *opportunity assessment* is designed for the vast majority of product work, which ranges from a simple optimization to a feature to a medium-sized project.

2. A *customer letter* is designed for larger projects or initiatives that often have multiple goals and a more complicated desired outcome.

3. A *startup canvas* for those times you're creating an entirely new product line or a new business.

Note that these techniques are not mutually exclusive. You may find it useful to do both an opportunity assessment and a customer letter, for example.

Problems versus Solutions

There is an underlying theme you'll see in all framing techniques, and the reason is that it's just human nature for people to think and talk in terms of *solutions* rather than the underlying *problems*. This applies especially to users and customers but also applies to stakeholders in our business, other company execs, and if we're honest with ourselves, it very often applies to us as well.

(continued)

(continued)

This problem famously applies to startup founders. Founders will often stew on a potential solution for month, if not years, before they get the funding and the nerve to pursue it.

> *More often than not, our initial solutions don't solve the problem—at least not in a way that can power a successful business.*

But one of the most important lessons in our industry is to *fall in love with the problem, not the solution.*

Why is this so important? Because, more often than not, our initial solutions don't solve the problem—at least not in a way that can power a successful business. It usually takes trying out several different approaches to a solution before we find one that solves the underlying problem.

This is another reason why typical product roadmaps are so problematic. They're lists of features and projects where each feature or project is a possible solution. Somebody believes that feature will solve the problem or it wouldn't be on the roadmap, but it's all too possible they are wrong. It's not their fault—there's just no way to know at the stage it's put on the roadmap.

However, there very likely is a legitimate problem behind that potential solution, and it's our job in the product organization to tease out the underlying problem and ensure that whatever solution we deliver solves that underlying problem.

A small amount of time up front framing the problem to be solved—and communicating this framing—can make a dramatic difference in the results.

35

Opportunity Assessment Technique

An opportunity assessment is an extremely simple technique but can save you a lot of time and grief.

The idea is to answer four key questions about the discovery work you are about to undertake:

1. What business objective is this work intended to address? (*Objective*)

2. How will you know if you've succeeded? (*Key results*)

3. What problem will this solve for our customers? (*Customer problem*)

4. What type of customer are we focused on? (*Target market*)

Business Objective

The first question should map to one or more of your team's assigned objectives. For example, if you've been asked to focus on the problem of growth, to reduce the time it takes for a new customer to onboard, or to reduce the percentage of customers that churn each month, then we want to be clear that this work will address at least one of our assigned problems.

Key Results

We want to know at the outset what the measure of success is. For example, if we're trying to reduce churn, would a 1 percent improvement be considered excellent or would be it be considered a waste of time? The second question should map to at least one of the *key results* assigned to our product team.

Customer Problem

Everything we do is, of course, intended to benefit our own company in some way or we wouldn't do

> *We want to keep the focus on our customers.*

it. But we want to keep the focus on our customers, and this question will clearly articulate the problem we want to solve for our customers. We occasionally do something to help internal users, so if that's the case we can call that out here. But even then, we try to tie it back to the benefits to our end customers.

Target Market

So much product work fails because it tries to please everyone and ends up pleasing no one. This question is intended to make it very clear to the product team who the primary intended beneficiary of this work is. Normally, this is a particular type of user or customer. It might be described as a user or customer persona, a specific target market, or a specific job to be done.

There are other factors you may want to consider when assessing an opportunity, depending on the nature of the opportunity, but I consider these four questions to be the bare minimum. You need to ensure that every member of your product team knows and understands the answers to these four questions before you jump into your product discovery work.

Answering these questions is the responsibility of the product manager, and it normally takes a few minutes to prepare these answers. But then the product manager needs to share them with her product team and with key stakeholders to ensure you are on the same page.

One important caveat: Sometimes the CEO or another senior leader will explain that there's something beyond normal product work that needs to be done. Realize that there are sometimes strategic reasons for doing specific product work, such as support a partnership. If it happens a lot, then that's a different issue, but it's usually infrequent. If that's the case, don't stress over it. Just give the team as much context as you can—these four questions may still be relevant.

36

Customer Letter Technique

For smaller and more typically sized efforts, the opportunity assessment is usually sufficient. But when embarking on a somewhat larger effort, there may in fact be multiple reasons, several customer problems to be solved, or business objectives to be tackled. To communicate the value effectively, it may take more than the four questions listed in the previous chapter.

A typical example of an effort of this size would be a redesign. There are likely several objectives in the redesign, and maybe it is intended to both improve the experience for current customers and perform better for new customers.

One of my favorite technology-powered product companies is Amazon. They have consistently innovated—including several truly disruptive innovations—and have shown they can continue to do this at scale. In my view, there are many reasons for this ongoing product success, from leadership, to talent, to culture, and especially to their sincere passion for taking care of customers. But there are a few

techniques that are central to how
Amazon builds product, and one of
them is referred to as the *working backward* process, where you
start the effort with a pretend press
release.

> *When embarking on a
> somewhat larger effort,
> there may in fact be multiple
> reasons, several customer
> problems to be solved, or
> business objectives to be
> tackled.*

The idea is that the product
manager frames the work ahead of
the team by writing an imagined
press release of what it would be like once this product launches. How
does it improve the life of our customers? What are the real benefits
to them? You've all read a press release before—the only difference is
that this is entirely imagined. It is describing a future state we want
to create.

It's so tempting for product teams to immediately slip into an enu-
meration of all the features they plan to build, with little real thought
into the actual benefits for our customers. This technique is intended
to counter that and to keep the team focused on the outcome, not the
output.

The actual reader of this press release is the product team,
related or impacted teams, and leadership. It's a terrific evangelism
technique—if people don't see the value after reading the press release,
then the product manager has more work to do, or perhaps should
reconsider the effort.

Some people also consider this a demand-validation technique
(if you can't get your team excited, maybe it's not worth doing). It's only
validating demand or value with your colleagues rather than with real
customers, however, so I think of it primarily as a framing technique.

In any case, Walker Lockhart, a former long-time Amazonian
who joined Nordstrom a couple of years ago, shared with me a variation of this technique that was developed and refined at Nordstrom.

The idea is that rather than communicate the benefits in a press
release format, you describe them in the format of a customer letter written from the hypothetical perspective of one of your product's
well-defined user or customer personas.

The letter—sent to the CEO from a very happy and impressed
customer—explains why he or she is so happy and grateful for the new
product or redesign. The customer describes how it has changed or

improved his or her life. The letter also includes an imagined congratulatory response from the CEO to the product team explaining how this has helped the business.

I hope you can see that this customer letter variation is very similar to Amazon's imagined press release, and it is intended to drive much the same type of thinking. A press release version includes a customer quote as well.

I like this customer letter variation even better than the press release style for a couple of reasons. First, the press release format is a bit dated. The press release doesn't play the role it used to in our industry, so it's not something that everyone is familiar with. Second, I think the customer letter does an even better job of creating empathy for the customer's current pain and more clearly emphasizes to the team how their efforts can help the lives of these customers.

I will also admit that I love actual customer letters. I find them to be extremely motivating. And it's worth noting that even when a customer letter is critical of the product, it helps the team to understand the problem viscerally, and they often feel compelled to find a way to help.

37

Startup Canvas Technique

So far, we've explored techniques for typical-sized, smaller efforts like adding a new feature, or medium to large-sized efforts like a redesign. Those cover most of what product teams actually work on.

However, another especially difficult situation requires a more comprehensive framing technique. This is an early stage startup, where you are trying to figure out a new product that can power a new business, or, for those that work at an enterprise size company, when you're asked to tackle an all-new business opportunity for the company.

In other words, you're not being asked to improve an existing product, you're being asked to invent an entirely new product.

In this situation, you have a much broader set of risks, including validating your value proposition, figuring out how you intend to make money, how you plan to get this product out to your customers and sell to them, how much it will cost to produce and sell this product, and what you will measure to track your progress—not to mention determining whether the market is large enough to sustain a business.

For decades, people would create thick business plans to try to highlight these topics and how they intended to tackle them. But many people, including me, have written about the many reasons those old business plans were often more harmful than helpful.

> *You're not being asked to improve an existing product, you're being asked to invent an entirely new product.*

A startup canvas, its close cousins the business model canvas, and the lean canvas are intended to be lightweight tools to call out these risks early and encourage the team to tackle them up front.

I much prefer the startup canvas to old-style business plans, but I have also observed that many startup teams still spend too much time on the canvas and keep postponing that pesky little problem of discovering a solution that people want to buy (see the box "The Biggest Risk").

You can use a canvas for any product change, no matter the size, but you would likely quickly find that, once you have an existing product and business, the majority of the canvas doesn't change and is only duplicated. You already have a sales or distribution model. You already have a monetization strategy. You have a well-defined cost structure. You are mainly trying to create more value in your solution. In that case, it probably makes sense for you to look at one of the earlier framing techniques.

That said, you can use the startup canvas for simpler work, especially if you have a new product manager. The startup canvas can help that new product manager get a good holistic understanding of her product and understand the key areas of the affected business.

The Biggest Risk

One of the things I like about a startup canvas is that it helps to quickly highlight the key assumptions and major risks facing a startup or a significant new product in an existing business. This is a good thing. The idea is to tackle the biggest risks first. At least that's the theory.

In practice, I keep running into entrepreneurs and product leaders who are focused on secondary risks rather than primary risks.

(continued)

(continued)

I think this is at least partly because risk is subjective and hard to quantify. So, depending on your perspective, you may think some risk is secondary when I think it is primary.

> *It's human nature for people to focus more on those areas they feel they can control and are knowledgeable about.*

Mostly, however, I think the major reason is that it's human nature for people to focus more on those areas they feel they can control and are knowledgeable about.

So, let's say your startup founder is someone who comes from a business background, probably trained as an MBA. He or she is likely acutely aware of the risks associated with coming up with a good business model. They're often focused on unique value proposition, pricing, channels, and costs. These are all real risks, which are part of assessing *business viability*.

But, I will often have to sit these people down and explain that, while these are real risks, they are largely academic at this stage. And then I try to point them at what, in my experience, is the biggest reason that startups and new products fail.

You're probably thinking that I'm speaking of market risk—that the new product is focused on solving a problem that customers just don't care enough about. This is a very real risk, and one that's responsible for its share of failed efforts, but I argue this is not usually the most significant risk.

I need to mention a couple caveats here.

First, I have to say that the vast majority of the teams I meet are not solving truly new problems. They are working on long-standing problems with long-proven markets. What's different about the startup or product is their approach to solving the problem (their solution), most often—and increasingly—because they are leveraging newly available technology to solve the problem in an innovative way.

Second, if the market is indeed new, then today the techniques we have for validating demand have never been better. If you don't use

(continued)

(continued)

these techniques, you proceed at your own peril. This is an especially egregious mistake because the techniques are not expensive in terms of money and time, so there's just no excuse not to do this.

I believe the major risk facing most efforts is *value risk*. On a startup canvas, this shows up under solution risk—discovering a compelling solution to customers. *A solution that your customers will choose to buy and use.*

This is generally hard enough but realize that to get someone to switch to our new product, it's not enough that it's comparable (sometimes referred to as feature parity), it must be *demonstrably and substantially better*. This is a high bar.

However, if you've created a canvas before, you know that there's precious little in there about the solution. The official rationale for that is that it's far too easy to fall in love with your particular approach and lock yourself in prematurely. In fairness, this is a very real issue with teams. I see this behavior frequently. But a consequence of this meager representation of the solution in a canvas is that it plays to the tendency of many to focus on those risks they feel more comfortable with and leave the solution as "an exercise for the engineers."

Rather than delegating or deferring figuring out the solution, we need to embrace product discovery as the most important core competency of the startup.

Look, if you can discover a solution that your customers love, then you can tackle the risks of monetization and scale. However, without that solution, the rest of your work is very likely going to be wasted. So, whether your constrained resource is cash or management's patience, you need to make sure you primarily use your time to discover a winning solution. Get that risk resolved first and then you can focus on the other risks.

The point is that you don't need to spend your time doing pricing optimization testing, sales tools, marketing programs, and cutting costs, until and unless you have discovered a truly valuable product.

Discovery Planning Techniques

Overview

Now that we've framed our discovery work, we're ready to jump in and start figuring out solutions. For complicated product efforts, it often helps to have some way to scope out and plan your discovery efforts.

In this section, I describe two of my favorite discovery-planning techniques. One is simple (story maps), and the other is fairly complicated (customer discovery program), but they are both remarkably powerful and effective.

I don't want to scare you away from a technique just because it's a lot of work. I often tell product teams that if they could only pick a single technique, the one I'd recommend is the customer discovery program. Yes, it's a lot of time and effort—especially on the shoulders of the product manager—but it's my favorite leading indicator of future success. I attribute much of the success in my own career to this technique.

38

Story Map Technique

Story maps are one of the most generally useful techniques I know. They are essentially a framing and planning technique, but they are just as useful for ideation. They are also used as a design technique when working on prototypes, and they are great for communicating with your team and stakeholders. They also play a very practical role in managing and organizing your work. Further, a story map is helpful throughout product discovery and delivery.

I think you'll agree that's a lot of benefits. But the best part is how simple it is.

The origin of story maps came from frustration with the typical flat backlog of user stories. There's no context, just a prioritized list of stories. How can the team know how one story fits in with the big picture? What does it mean to even prioritize at that granularity with so little context? And what set of stories constitutes a meaningful milestone or a release?

Jeff Patton, one of the early Agile thinkers, was frustrated by this, so he leveraged some proven UX design techniques, and adapted them to Agile concepts and introduced user story maps.

These are two-dimensional maps, in which major user activities are arrayed along the horizontal dimension, loosely ordered by time from left to right. So, if there are a dozen major user activities, they would be along the top from left to right, generally in the order you would do them—or at least, if you were describing the overall system to someone else, the order in which you'd describe them.

> *Many teams I know consider a high-fidelity user prototype and a story map as their go-to techniques.*

Along the vertical dimension, we have a progressive level of detail. As we flesh out each major activity into sets of user tasks, we add stories for each of those tasks. The critical tasks are higher vertically than the optional tasks.

If you lay out your system this way, you can, at a glance, get the holistic view and consider where to draw the line in terms of different releases and their associated objectives.

Now each story has context. The entire team can see how it fits in with the other stories. And not just as a snapshot in time. The team can see how the system is expected to grow over time.

We can use this story map to frame our prototypes, and then as we get feedback on our prototypes and learn how people interact with our product ideas, we can easily update the story map to serve as a living reflection of the prototypes. As we finalize our discovery work and progress into delivery, the stories from the map move right into the product backlog.

Many teams I know consider a high-fidelity user prototype and a story map as their go-to techniques.

Another must-read book for product managers: *User Story Mapping: Discover the Whole Story, Build the Right Product*, by Jeff Patton (O'Reilly Media, 2014).

39

Customer Discovery Program Technique

Our job in the product organization is to create products that can sustain a business. Make no mistake about it: Everything depends on strong products.

Without strong products, our marketing programs require customer acquisition costs that are too high; our sales organization is forced to get "creative," which drives up cost of sales, lengthens the sales cycle, and puts downward pressure on price; and our customer success organization is forced to take it on the chin every day with frustrated customers.

The downward spiral continues because the sales organization loses a lot of deals when they try to compete with a weak product. So, what do they do? They start yelling at you about all the features you don't have, and the competitor they lost to who does, which typically just makes the bad situation even worse. And then you start complaining about working at a sales-driven company.

Many of you may be thinking I've just described your company. Sadly, I find this to be the state of affairs in far too many companies, especially those with either a direct sales organization or an advertising sales organization.

This entire book, in one way or another, is intended to prevent or correct this situation. However, in this chapter, I talk about what I consider one of the most powerful techniques we have to ensure and prove we have a strong, viable product and prevent the situation I've just described.

The Power of Reference Customers

First, we need to talk about the nearly magical power of a happy reference customer.

Let's be clear about what it means to be a *reference customer*: This is a *real* customer (not friends or family), who is running your product in *production* (not a trial or prototype), who has paid *real money*

> *There are few things more powerful to a product organization than reference customers.*

for the product (it wasn't given away to entice them to use it), and, most important, who is willing to *tell others* how much they love your product (voluntarily and sincerely).

Please believe me when I say that there are few things more powerful to a product organization than reference customers. It is the single best sales tool you can provide to your sales and marketing organization, and it completely changes the dynamics between the product organization and the rest of the company.

Ask any good salesperson the single best tool you can provide to help her do her job, and she'll say, "happy reference customers."

If you find that you're constantly frustrated by having to react to sales and the latest big-deal prospect they've managed to bring in, this is how you turn the situation around.

Without reference customers, it's very hard for the sales team to know where the real product/market fit is. And remember—they have a quota and are paid by commission. So, without good examples, they will sell however and whatever they can. Without reference customers, this situation is not their fault—it's *your* fault.

> *We are discovering and developing a set of reference customers in parallel with discovering and developing the actual product.*

The reason I love the customer discovery program technique so much is because it is designed to produce these reference customers.

We are discovering and developing a set of reference customers in parallel with discovering and developing the actual product.

I will warn you that this technique takes substantial effort, primarily on the part of the product manager. I wish it were easier. But I will also say that if you do this technique, I consider it the *single best leading indicator of future product success*.

I will also say that this technique is not new, although every few years some influential person in the product world rediscovers its power and it gets attention once again. It also goes by multiple names. In any case, I'm convinced that everyone would do the technique if it didn't require so much actual work.

There are four main variations of this technique for four different situations:

1. Building products for businesses
2. Building platform products (e.g., public APIs)
3. Building customer-enabling tools used by employees of your company
4. Building products for consumers

The core concept is the same for all four variations, but there are some differences. I'll describe the variation for businesses first and then describe the differences for each of the other uses.

I also need to point out that you would not do this program for small efforts like features or minor projects. This is for larger efforts. Good examples would be creating a new product or business, taking an existing product to a new market or new geography or a redesign of a product.

The basic driver behind this technique is that, with a significant new product, the most common objection is that prospective customers want to see that other companies, like themselves, are already successfully using the product. They want to see the reference customers. In general, the more reference customers the better but too few, and the prospective customer is worried that the product is a special and only works for those one or two customers.

For products and services aimed at businesses, I was taught years ago that the key number is six reference customers. This is not meant to be statistically significant—it is meant to instill confidence—and I have found that number has held up over time. Again, more than six would be even better, but we shoot for six because each one is a lot of work.

Single Target Market

Now these are not just any six customers. We are looking to develop six reference customers in our specific target market or segment, so, the idea is to find six similar customers. If you end up targeting two or three customers from two or three different markets, this program will not give you the focus you want and need.

In the earlier chapters on product vision and strategy, we talked about the product strategy of pursuing a product vision by tackling one vertical market after another. For example, first develop six references for the financial services industry, then six for the manufacturing industry, and so on. Or you can expand geographically in this same manner (for example, first develop six references for the United States, six for Germany, and then six for Brazil, and so on).

I do my best to persuade teams to not launch a product in the marketplace until after they have those six reference customers. We don't want to turn on the sales or marketing machine until we have evidence that we can help them be successful, and the reference customers are our best evidence.

The concept behind this technique is to focus on developing this set of reference customers for a specific target market, which then makes it easy for sales to go after those specific types of customers. Once we have those reference customers for that initial target market, we can move on to expanding the product to meet the needs of the next target market.

Recruiting the Prospective Reference Customers

We want to end with six reference customers, so we'll typically recruit between six and eight in case one or two turn out to be not a match or unavailable. We need them to be from the specific target market we are going after. They may be from your existing customer base, prospects, or a blend.

We are looking for prospective customers that truly feel the pain and are near desperate for the solution we want to build. If they could find a solution that worked for them elsewhere, they would have already bought it.

However, it's also important we screen out technologists. These people are mainly interested because of the technology, not because they desperately need the business value.

We need them to have people and time willing to work closely with us. They need to be willing to spend time with the product team, testing out early prototypes and helping the team ensure the product works well for them. If possible, we would like them to be well-recognized marquee names, because that will be of the most value to the sales and marketing staff.

Coming up with the right set is normally something the product manager does in tight collaboration with the product marketing manager.

The Relationship

The benefit to the prospective customer is that they get real input, not lip service, to the solution—and, most important, they get a solution that truly works for them.

The benefit to the product team is that you get ready access to a set of users and customers that you can go deep with and figure out a solution that will work for them. They've provided you access to their users. They have agreed to test early versions. And, what's really important, they have agreed to buy the product and serve as a public reference *if* the resulting product works for them.

It's critical to explain to each prospective member of the program that your job is to come up with a *general product*—something your company can successfully sell to a large number of customers. You're not trying to build a custom solution that only works for that one company (and they wouldn't want that in any case as they would be left with unsupported, dead-end software). You are, however, deeply committed to coming up with a product that works extremely well for them and just a handful of other companies.

Further, your job as product manager is not to put in the features that all six companies request. While that would be much easier, that would yield an awful product. Your job is to dive deep with each of the six customers and identify a *single solution* that works well for all six customers.

There are a number of important points to consider with this technique.

Not everyone agrees with me on this, but I don't personally like the customer to pay in advance to participate in this program. That makes this a different type of relationship. You want a *partner* in coming up with the product. You do not want to build a custom solution just for them, and you're not a custom project shop. You can take their money after you deliver them a product they love. That said, if you're a very early stage startup with little cash, you may have to bend this rule just a bit. A compromise is to have them put the money into escrow.

If you are working on an important and difficult problem, you will likely be overwhelmed with customers that want to participate. It really is a good deal, and customers know this. If you have a sales organization, they'll try to use this as a bargaining chip, and the result is that you'll be leaned on to include many more customers than you can handle. This will take finesse at times, but it's important that the members of the customer discovery program be the right set, and no more than eight. However, it's no problem also having an early release program that is essentially unlimited for those customers that want the software early, but you determine aren't right for the customer discovery program.

Note that, in many cases, you'll get people who say they are extremely interested in this product, but they first want to see your references. When you explain you're looking to work with them to become one of those references, they will probably say they are just too busy, but to come back once you have the references. That's fine. They're a useful lead. But we are looking for those customers that are so hungry and desperate for a solution that they will absolutely make time for this. Every market has this segment.

That said, if you find you are having real trouble recruiting even four or five prospective customers for this effort, then it's very possible you're chasing a problem that isn't that important, and you will almost certainly have a very hard time selling this product. This is one of the very first reality checks (aka *demand validation*) to make sure you're spending your time on something worthwhile. If customers aren't interested in this problem, you may want to rethink your plans.

You need to make sure your customers are truly from your target market and not more than one target market. A big benefit of this program is focus, and that means the customers are from a single target market.

You will want to work with your product marketing manager to ensure that the prospective customer has permission from their marketing organization to serve as a public reference. You will also want to keep your product marketing partner continuously involved in this program as she can help turn your reference customer into some great sales tools and collateral. But, remember, it is your job to develop those actual reference customers—so be sure you deliver a product they love.

Think of these early prospective customers as development partners. You're in this together. You need to treat them as colleagues—open the kimono, you are helping each other. You'll find that the relationships you create can last for many years.

You will be interacting with these people throughout the effort—you'll be showing them prototypes and testing with their users, you'll be asking many detailed questions, and you'll be testing early versions in their environment.

Make sure you release the delivered product to these people *before* the general release, and make sure they are live and happy before the release. When you launch, they'll be ready to stand up for you.

Now let's consider the common variations of this program for different types of products.

Platform/API Products

For developer products, the program is very much like the one for businesses, but the main difference is that we work with the development teams (engineers and product managers) that will use our APIs to get them successfully using our product. The result of the program is a set of reference *applications* rather than reference customers. We focus on the successful applications created with our APIs.

Customer-Enabling Tools

For customer-enabling tools, such as a new dashboard for your customer service agents, we pick six to eight well-respected, influential internal users/employees—the individuals that the other agents look up to as thought leaders—and we work closely with them to discover the necessary product. Obviously, they are not customers and not paying anything, but instead we ask them to work closely with us through product discovery to make this tool great. Once they believe that the product is ready, we ask them to tell their colleagues how much they love the new tool.

Consumer Products

For consumer products, the same general concept applies. But, rather than focusing on six businesses to work closely with (where we have access to many different users at each customer), we instead focus on a somewhat larger number of consumers (on the order of 10–50) that we engage with to get them to the point that they are loving our product.

It's important to emphasize that, for consumer products, we will need to supplement this program with much broader testing of our product ideas—typically with people that have never been exposed to the product. But it is often very helpful to have a smaller group of prospective users that we can go back to over time, and that's what this is for.

In terms of marketing, when a consumer decides to buy or use a product, they may not look at reference customers as a business purchaser would. But they are affected by social media, the press, and other influencers, and when the press does write a story about your product, the first thing they'll look for is real users.

Summary

While you can see this may be a lot of effort, especially for the product manager, this powerful technique help ensures that you're building a product that customers love.

Remember that this technique is not designed to discover the necessary product—that comes next. Rather, it is designed to give you direct access to the target customers where you'll find the product ideas necessary to generate reference customers.

Defining Product/Market Fit

There are many ways of defining this critically important concept of product/market fit. Unfortunately, most of them are largely subjective.

> *Product/market fit shows up in terms of happier customers, lower churn rates, shortened sales cycles, and rapid organic growth.*

It is true that product/market fit is one of those things that "you know it when you see it." It certainly shows up in terms of happier customers, lower churn rates, shortened sales cycles, and rapid organic growth. But the threshold for any of these can be tough to define.

Companies often spend countless hours debating what product/market fit should mean for them and whether they have achieved it.

One of the most common techniques for assessing product/market fit is known as the Sean Ellis test. This involves surveying

(continued)

(continued)

your users (those in your target market that have used the product recently, at least a couple times, and you know from the analytics that they've at least made it through to the core value of the product) and asking them how they'd feel if they could no longer use this product. (The choices are "very disappointed," "somewhat disappointed," "don't care," and "no longer relevant because I no longer use."). The general rule of thumb is that if more than 40 percent of the users would be "very disappointed," then there's a good chance you're at product/market fit.

While useful, as you might imagine there are lots of caveats here, depending on the type of product and the size of the sample. I like this test for consumer products and services, but for products for businesses, one of the reasons I like this customer discovery program so much is that I consider this a very practical and very effective definition of product/market fit.

If we can get to the point where we have six reference customers in a specific target market, we will typically declare product/market fit for that market.

Remember product/market fit does not mean that you are done with working on that product. Not even close. We will continue to improve that product continuously for years. However, once we have those six reference customers, we can aggressively and effectively sell that product to other customers in that market.

So, each reference customer is a truly significant milestone. But, for example, getting six reference customers in a given target market for a B2B company is perhaps the most significant, meaningful milestone business result for a product organization and something truly worth celebrating.

40

Profile: Martina Lauchengco of Microsoft

In 1993, Word 6.0 was the biggest release, feature-wise, Microsoft had ever produced.

In addition to all the new features, the team had another very large objective. Their code base had diverged, and it was extremely slow and costly for Microsoft to implement Word separately for each platform: Windows, DOS, and Mac. This code convergence effort was supposed to save Microsoft substantial development time, and—they tried to convince themselves—improve the offering since Word would have the same features on every platform.

It also meant that there was great pressure to get the release out so they could start to gain the efficiencies of a single code base.

At the time, Word for Mac was a relatively small market. It was only $60 million, versus Windows, which at that point was more than a $1 billion market. If you remember, back then Windows machines absolutely dominated, and the future of Apple was not a sure thing. However, the Mac community was also very vocal—with passionate fans of their platform—and this community had very little love for Microsoft.

PowerMacs were just hitting the market, which had significantly faster chips and more memory. Most of the team members were using those new computers because the Word 6.0 beta in its early days was just too slow on regular Macs. Of course, most of the Mac user base was not on new PowerMacs—they were on regular Macs. Hardware upgrade cycles were much slower then.

So, when Microsoft released the most "full-featured word processor ever for the Mac," it *crawled* on their Macs—we're talking two minutes just to start it up.

The community immediately started posting in newsgroups that Microsoft was trying to "kill the Mac." Hate mail started streaming in from everywhere, including e-mails directly to Bill Gates, who would forward them to the team with messages like "This is depressing MSFT's stock price. Fix it."

Enter Martina Lauchengco, a young product manager recently out of Stanford, whose job it was to help turn this around.

The team quickly learned that, while it may be a worthwhile objective to get to a common code base, it's an empty victory if the product that results is not good. Moreover, users choose their devices and platforms because they value what's *different*, not what's the same. From the customer's point of view, they would rather wait a little longer and have a better platform-specific solution, than simultaneously ship a generic product on all platforms.

The team ended up focusing hard on performance and taking advantage of what the Mac could do. They looked at when and how to load fonts, since Mac users tended to have so many more than Windows users, and ensuring all Mac keyboard shortcuts still worked.

They focused on word count—which is used 10 times a day by every press person—to make sure that it was lightning fast, as the press used the feature as their performance barometer. They even made it faster than the feature on Windows.

The result was that in a couple of months they produced a 6.1 release that was sent to every registered user with an apology letter—signed by Martina—along with a discount coupon for future purchases.

The release succeeded in fixing the perception problems, but more important, it genuinely made the version dramatically better for the Macintosh. It was a product the Mac team could be proud of and what the team felt they should have delivered to market in the first place.

> *This is a good example of how hard it can be to do the right thing for the customer, often in the face of massive pressures. But that's exactly what strong product managers figure out how to do.*

This is a good example of how hard it can be to do the right thing for the customer, often in the face of massive pressures. But that's exactly what strong product managers figure out how to do.

In subsequent years, not only did Microsoft once again decide to diverge the code base, they completely separated the teams into different buildings and business units and had them fully embrace all things Mac. Strategically, it was a complete 180.

It's hard to estimate how important this was to both Microsoft and Apple. Even today, more than 20 years later, many businesses and consumers consider Word and the rest of Office absolutely essential to using their Mac for business and personal use. What started then became a multibillion-dollar win for both Apple and Microsoft. There are more than *1 billion Macs and PCs* running Office around the world.

Martina has gone on to have a remarkable career in both product management and product marketing. From Microsoft she went on to Netscape, where she was responsible for marketing of the Netscape browser, and then Loudcloud. And now I'm happy to say she's been my partner at SVPG for more than a decade, and she also teaches marketing at University of California, Berkeley.

Let me also add that there are few things as powerful as a marketing person who's also strong at product. The combination is amazing.

Discovery Ideation Techniques

Overview

There are, of course, any number of techniques for generating product ideas. I really haven't met many ideation techniques I haven't liked. But to me, the more relevant question is, "How do we generate the types of ideas that are likely to truly help us solve the hard business problems that our leaders have asked us to focus on right now?"

Remarkably, in the vast majority of companies (not the ones that are good at product), the actual product teams don't do much ideation themselves. This is because what's really going on is that the ideas are already handed to the product teams in the form of prioritized features on product roadmaps, where most of the items on those roadmaps are coming either from requests from big customers (or prospective customers), or from company stakeholders or execs. Unfortunately, these are rarely the quality of ideas we're looking for.

In general, if the product team is given actual business problems to solve rather than solutions, and the product team does their job and interacts directly and frequently with actual users and customers, then getting a sufficient quantity and quality of product ideas is not really a problem.

I have some favorite techniques that consistently deliver to the team very promising and very relevant product ideas.

One important caveat, though. If you use these techniques, I am fairly certain you will get very excited by many of the

How do we generate the types of ideas that are likely to truly help us solve the hard business problems that our leaders have asked us to focus on right now?

ideas you discover. But that doesn't mean you should just go ahead and build them. In most cases, we will still need to test them to ensure they are valuable and usable for our customers, are feasible for our engineers, and are viable for our business.

41

Customer Interviews

The customer interview is the most basic technique I'll discuss in this book. I wish I didn't need to include it because I'd like to be able to take it for granted that product managers already know how to do this well and do it frequently.

However, the reality is that this is often not the case. Or, if customer interviews are happening, the product manager is not present, so the learnings are not understood viscerally or taken as seriously as they need to be (see Discovery Principle #10 on shared learning).

But no question, this is one of the most powerful and important skills for any product manager and very often the source or inspiration for many breakthrough product ideas. Later, when we discuss techniques for testing your product ideas qualitatively, these skills will be a prerequisite.

There are many forms of customer interviews, so this is not really a single technique. Some are informal and some are more formal. Some have a user research methodology behind them (one of my favorites is the *contextual inquiry*), and others are more about just getting out of the building and learning what you don't know.

But in every user or customer interaction, we always have the opportunity to learn some valuable insights. Here's what I'm always trying to understand:

> *This is one of the most powerful and important skills for any product manager and very often the source or inspiration for many breakthrough product ideas.*

- Are your customers who you think they are?
- Do they really have the problems you think they have?
- How does the customer solve this problem today?
- What would be required for them to switch?

Now there are lots of ways to get these answers, and if you have access to a user researcher, you would normally follow their lead. Here are some tips for getting the most out of these learning opportunities:

Frequency. Establish a regular cadence of customer interviews. This should not be a once-in-a-while thing. A bare minimum would be two to three hours of customer interviews per week, every week.

Purpose. You are not trying to prove anything during these interviews, one way or the other. You're just trying to understand and learn quickly. This mindset is critical and needs to be sincere.

Recruiting users and customers. I talk much more about this when we discuss the usability testing technique, but for now, be sure to talk primarily to people in your intended target market. You're looking for about an hour of their time.

Location. It's always amazing to see customers in their native habitat. There's so much to learn just by observing their environment. But it's also fine to meet them somewhere convenient or have them come to your office. If you need to do this over a video call, that's not as good, but much better than not doing at all.

Preparation. Be clear beforehand what problem it is you think they have, and think about how you'll either confirm or contradict that.

Who should attend. My favorite is to bring three people to these interviews: the product manager, the product designer, and one of the engineers from the team (we normally rotate among those that want to attend). Usually, the designer drives (because they've usually been trained how to do this well), the product manager takes notes, and the developer observes.

Interview. Work to keep things natural and informal, ask open-ended questions, and try to learn what they're doing today (not so much what they *wish* they were doing, although that's also interesting).

Afterward. Debrief with your colleagues to see if you've all heard the same things and had the same learnings. If you made any promises to the customer during that session, be sure you keep them.

I would argue that this hour consistently yields a great return on your time. It's critical to learn the answers to these key questions. However, I am a big fan of taking the opportunity of a customer interview to also try out some of our product ideas. We do that after we've learned the answers to these key questions, but it's such a great opportunity I really like to take advantage of it.

Later, when we talk about testing usability and value, you will see the techniques for this. But for now, just know that you don't have to wrap up after the interview—you can follow it up with a user test of your latest product ideas.

This hour consistently yields a great return on your time.

42

Concierge Test Technique

A concierge test is one of my favorite techniques for quickly generating high-quality product ideas and, at the same time, working on developing the customer understanding and empathy that's so important for motivating the team and delivering strong solutions.

A *concierge test* is a relatively new name to describe an old but effective technique. The idea is that we do the customer's job for them—manually and personally. Just as if you went to a hotel concierge and asked if he could find you some theater tickets to a popular show. You don't really know the details of what that concierge is doing for you to get those tickets, but you do know that he is doing something.

With this technique, *you* become the concierge. You do what the user or customer needs done for them. You may have to ask them to train you first, but you are in their shoes doing the tasks they would do.

This is similar, but not the same, as spending some time with your customer service or customer success staff. That is also valuable, and often a good source of product ideas as well, but that is helping customers once they call with a problem.

A concierge test requires going out to the actual users and customers and asking them to show you how they work so that you can learn how to do their job, and so that you can work on providing them a much better solution.

A concierge test requires going out to the actual users and customers and asking them to show you how they work so that you can learn how to do their job, and so that you can work on providing them a much better solution.

If you are building a *customer-enabling* product, the users may be employees of your company, but the technique is the same—you go to these colleagues and ask them to teach you how they do their job.

Like the principle of shared learning, it is most valuable if the product manager, the product designer, and one of the engineers does the concierge test.

43

The Power of Customer Misbehavior

Historically, the two main approaches used by good teams to come up with product opportunities have been:

1. Try to assess the market opportunities and pick potentially lucrative areas where significant pain exists.
2. Look at what the technology or data enables—what's just now possible—and match that up with the significant pain.

You can think of the first as following the market, and the second as following the technology. Either way can get you to a winning product.

However, some of the most successful companies today have taken a third approach, and while it's not appropriate for every company, I would like to suggest that this is an extremely powerful technique that's largely underutilized and underappreciated in our industry.

This third alternative is to allow, and even encourage, our customers to use our products to solve problems other than what we planned for and officially support.

Mike Fisher, a longtime friend of mine, wrote a book called *The Power of Customer Misbehavior*. This

> *This technique is to allow, and even encourage, our customers to use our products to solve problems other than what we planned for and officially support.*

book tells the eBay and Facebook stories from a viral growth perspective, but there are several other very good examples in there, too.

From its earliest days, eBay has always had an "Everything Else" category. This is where people could buy and sell things that we at eBay couldn't anticipate people might want to trade. And while we anticipated a lot (there were and still are thousands of categories), some of the biggest innovations and biggest surprises came from monitoring what customers *wanted* to do.

We realized early on in the eBay situation that this was where much of the best innovation was happening, and we did everything we could think of to encourage and nurture customers using the eBay marketplace to be able to buy and sell nearly anything.

While the marketplace may have been originally designed to facilitate trading items like electronics and collectibles, soon people started trading concert tickets, fine art, and even cars. Today, amazingly, eBay is one of the largest used car companies in the world.

As you might imagine, there are some very significant differences between safely buying and transporting a car and buying a ticket that's good for one night and then worthless. But that work was only done after the demand had been established by enabling customers to transact in items and ways the team and the company didn't anticipate.

Some product people can get upset when they find customers using their products for unintended use cases. This concern is usually tied to the support obligations. I'm suggesting, however, that this special case can be very strategic and well worth the investment to support. If you find your customers using your product in ways you didn't predict, this is potentially very valuable information. Dig in a little and learn what problem they are trying to solve and why they believe your product might provide the right foundation. Do this enough and you'll soon see patterns and, potentially, some very big product opportunities.

The Power of Developer Misbehavior

While the eBay example was intended to be used by end users (buyers and sellers), this same concept is what's behind the trend toward exposing some or all of a product's services via programmatic interfaces (public APIs).

> *I consider developers to be one of the consistently best sources of truly innovative product ideas.*

With a public API, you are essentially saying to the developer community, "These are the things we can do—perhaps you can leverage these services to do something amazing that we couldn't anticipate ourselves."

Facebook's platform strategy is a good example of this. They opened up access to their social graph to discover the types of things that developers might be able to do once they could leverage this asset.

I have been a long-time fan of public APIs as a part of a company's product strategy. I consider developers to be one of the consistently best sources of truly innovative product ideas. Developers are in the best position to see what's just now possible, and so many innovations are powered by these insights.

CHAPTER

44

Hack Days

There are many variations of hack days, but in this chapter, I describe one of my favorite techniques to quickly get a range of high-potential ideas that are focused on solving a pressing business or customer problem.

The two main types of hack days are directed and undirected. In an *undirected* hack day, people can explore whatever product ideas they like, so long as it's at least loosely related to the mission of the company.

In a *directed* hack day, there's a customer problem (for example, something is really difficult to learn and use, or it takes too long to do) or business objective we've been assigned (for example, "Reduce the

> *This is one of my favorite techniques for building a team of missionaries rather than mercenaries.*

customer churn rate" or "Increase customer lifetime value"), and we ask people from the product teams to self-organize and work on any ideas they like that might address this objective.

The goal is for the self-organizing groups to explore their ideas and create some form of prototype that can be evaluated, and if appropriate, tested on actual users.

There are two major benefits to these directed hack days. The first is practical, as the technique facilitates the inclusion of engineers at ideation. I've mentioned several times in this book that many of the best ideas come from the engineers on the team, and we need to ensure this is happening. It should be happening on an ongoing basis, but this technique will ensure it happens.

The second benefit is cultural. This is one of my favorite techniques for building a team of missionaries rather than mercenaries. The engineers, if they haven't already, are now diving much deeper into the business context and playing a much larger role in terms of innovation.

Discovery Prototyping Techniques

Overview

Prototypes of various forms have been around for as long as we've been applying technology to solve problems. Per the famous Fred Brooks quote, "Plan to throw one away; you will, anyhow."

While Fred's quote is as relevant today as when it was first published (in 1975!), many things have changed, not the least

> *"Plan to throw one away; you will, anyhow."*

of which is that the tools and techniques we have for developing prototypes and testing them have progressed dramatically.

That said, I continue to find teams, and even people I would consider thought leaders, that have a very narrow interpretation of what is meant by the term *prototype*.

When I press people, what I typically find is that they associate the term prototype with the type that they were first exposed to. If the first one you saw was used to test for feasibility, that's what you think of. If the first one you saw was used for usability testing, that's what you think of.

But there are in fact many very different forms of prototypes, each with different characteristics and each suited to testing different things. And, yes, some people get themselves into trouble trying to use the wrong type of prototype for the job at hand.

In this overview, I highlight the major classes of prototypes, and in the chapters that follow, I go into depth on each of them.

Feasibility Prototypes

These are written by engineers to address technical feasibility risks during product discovery—before we decide whether something is feasible. Sometimes, the engineers are trying out a new technology. Sometimes it's a new algorithm. Often it is about assessing performance. The idea is for the developer to write just enough code to be able to address the feasibility risk.

User Prototypes

User prototypes are simulations. There is a wide spectrum of user prototypes—from those intentionally designed to look like wireframes sketched out on paper (referred to as *low-fidelity user prototypes*) all the way up to those that look and feel like the real thing (referred to as *high-fidelity user prototypes*), where it can be difficult to tell it's just a simulation.

Live-Data Prototypes

Live-data prototypes are a little more complicated to explain, but they are a critically important tool for several situations. The main purpose of a *live-data prototype* is to collect actual data so we can prove something, or at least gather some evidence—normally to find out whether an idea (a feature, a design approach, a workflow) really works. This typically means two things. First, we need the prototype to access our live data sources, and second, we need to be able to send live traffic—in enough quantity to get some useful data—to the prototype.

The key is that we don't want to have to build, test, and deploy a commercially viable product to do this. That would take far too long, cost far too much, and very likely yield huge waste. A live-data prototype costs a small fraction of what it would cost to build a commercially viable product, which is what makes this such a powerful tool.

Hybrid Prototypes

There are also many hybrids, which combine aspects of the other types. For example, when working on search and recommendations in which we're focusing on relevance, we may need to have the prototype access live-data sources, but we don't need to be able to send live traffic. In this case, we're not trying to prove anything, but we can learn a great deal by observing and discussing the results with the users.

Remember that product discovery is all about coming up with the fastest, cheapest way to test out our ideas. So, depending on your particular idea and situation, you'll want to pick the flavor of prototype that best meets your needs.

While we all might have our favorites, if you are competing against good product teams, you are going to need to be skilled at each of these.

45

Principles of Prototypes

As discussed in Chapter 44, there are many forms of prototypes. The best choice for you depends on the particular risk being tackled and the type of product. But all forms of prototypes have certain characteristics and benefits in common. Here are five key principles behind their use.

1. The overarching purpose of any form of prototype is to learn something at a much lower cost in terms of time and effort than building out a product. All forms of prototype should require *at least* an order of magnitude less time and effort as the eventual product.

2. Realize that one of the key benefits of any form of prototype is to force you to think through a problem at a substantially deeper level than if we just talk about it or write something down. This is why the very act of creating a prototype so often exposes major issues otherwise left uncovered until much later.

3. Similarly, a prototype is also a powerful tool for team collaboration. Members of the product team and business partners can all experience the prototype to develop shared understanding.

> *The overarching purpose of any form of prototype is to learn something at a much lower cost in terms of time and effort than building out a product.*

4. There are many different possible levels of *fidelity* for a prototype. The fidelity primarily refers to how realistic the prototype looks. There is no such thing as one appropriate level of fidelity. Sometimes we don't need the prototype to look realistic at all, and other times it needs to be very realistic. The principle is that we create the *right* level of fidelity for its intended purpose, and we acknowledge that lower fidelity is faster and cheaper than higher fidelity, so we only do higher fidelity when we need to.

5. The primary purpose of a prototype is to tackle one or more product risks (value, usability, feasibility, or viability) in discovery; however, in many cases, the prototype goes on to provide a second benefit, which is to communicate to the engineers and the broader organization what needs to be built. This is often referred to as *prototype as spec*. In many cases, the prototype is sufficient for this, but in other cases—especially when the engineers are not co-located or when the product is especially complex—the prototype will likely need to be supplemented with additional details (usually, use cases, business rules, and acceptance criteria).

46

Feasibility Prototype Technique

M ost of the time your engineers will review your product ideas and tell you that they have no real concerns about feasibility. This is because they have likely built similar things many times before.

However, there are several situations wherein your engineers may identify a significant feasibility risk involved in solving a particular problem they are working on. Common examples include:

- Algorithm concerns
- Performance concerns
- Scalability concerns
- Fault tolerance concerns
- Use of a technology the team has not used before
- Use of a third-party component or service the team has not used before

- Use of a legacy system the team has not used before
- Dependency on new or related changes by other teams

> *The idea is to write just enough code to mitigate the feasibility risk.*

The main technique used for tackling these types of risks is for one or more of the engineers to build a *feasibility prototype*.

An engineer will create the feasibility prototype because it is typically code (as opposed to most prototypes created by special-purpose tools intended to be used by product designers). A feasibility prototype is a long way from a commercially shippable product—the idea is to write just enough code to mitigate the feasibility risk. This typically represents just a small percentage of the work for the eventual shippable product.

Further, most of the time the feasibility prototype is intended to be throwaway code—it's okay and normal to be quick and dirty with this. It is intended to be just enough to collect the data, for example, to show that performance would likely be acceptable or not. There is usually no user interface, error handling, or any of the typical work involved in productization.

In my experience, building a feasibility prototype requires usually just a day or two of time. If you're exploring a major new technology, such as a new approach leveraging machine-learning technology, then the feasibility prototype could very well take significantly longer.

The amount of time the feasibility prototype is estimated to take comes from the engineers, but whether or not the team takes that time depends on the product manager's judgment call as to whether it's worth pursuing this idea. She might say many other approaches to this problem don't have the technology feasibility risk, so she would rather skip this idea.

While it's the engineers who do this feasibility prototyping work, it is considered discovery work and not delivery work. It's done as part of deciding whether to even pursue this particular approach or idea.

In terms of lessons learned, I have seen many teams proceed to delivery without adequately considering the feasibility risk. Whenever you hear stories of product teams that grossly underestimated the amount of work required to build and deliver something, this is usually the underlying reason.

It may be that the engineers were simply too inexperienced with their estimates, that the engineers and product manager had an insufficient understanding of what was going to be needed, or that the product manager did not give the engineers sufficient time to truly investigate.

47

User Prototype Technique

A *user prototype*—one of the most powerful tools in product discovery—is a simulation. Smoke and mirrors. It's all a façade. There is nothing behind the curtain. In other words, if you have a user prototype of an e-commerce site, you can enter your credit card information as many times as you want—you won't actually be buying anything.

There is a wide range of user prototypes.

At one end of the spectrum are low-fidelity user prototypes. A low-fidelity user prototype doesn't look real—it is essentially an interactive wireframe. Many teams use these as a way to think through the product among themselves, but there are other uses as well.

Low-fidelity user prototypes, however, represent only one dimension of your product—the information and the workflow—there's nothing there about the impact of visual design or the differences caused by the actual data, to mention just a couple of important examples.

At the other end of the spectrum are high-fidelity user prototypes. A high-fidelity user prototype is still a simulation; however, now it looks and feels very real. In fact, with many good high-fidelity user prototypes, you need to look close to see that it's not real. The data you see is very realistic, but it's not real either—mostly meaning it's not live.

> *A user prototype is key to several types of validation and is also one of our most important communication tools.*

For example, if in my e-commerce user prototype example, I do a search for a particular type of mountain bike, it always comes back with the same set of mountain bikes. But if I look closely, they're not the actual bikes I asked for. And I notice that every time I search, it's always the same set of bikes no matter what price or style I specify.

If you are trying to test the relevance of the search results, this would not be the right tool for the job. But if you are trying to come up with a good overall shopping experience or figure out how people want to search for mountain bikes, this is probably more than adequate, and it's very quick and easy to create.

There are many tools for creating user prototypes—for every type of device, and for every level of fidelity. The tools are mainly developed for product designers. In fact, your product designer almost certainly already has one or more favorite user prototyping tools.

It's also the case that some designers prefer to hand-code their high-fidelity user prototypes, which is fine so long as they are fast, and they are willing to treat the prototype as disposable.

The big limitation of a user prototype is that it's not good for *proving* anything—like whether or not your product will sell.

Where a lot of novice product people go sideways is when they create a high-fidelity user prototype and they put it in front of 10 or 15 people who all say how much they love it. They think they've validated their product, but unfortunately, that's not how it works. People say all kinds of things and then go do something different.

We have much better techniques for validating value, so it's important that you understand what a user prototype is *not* appropriate for.

This is one of the most important techniques for product teams, so it is well worth developing your team's skills and experience in creating user prototypes at all levels of fidelity. As you'll see in the coming chapters, a user prototype is key to several types of validation and is also one of our most important communication tools.

48

Live-Data Prototype Technique

Sometimes, in order to address a major risk identified in discovery, we need to be able to collect some actual usage data. But we need to collect this evidence while in discovery, well before taking the time and expense of building an actual scalable and shippable product.

Some of my favorite examples of this are when applying game dynamics, search result relevance, many social features, and product funnel work.

This is the purpose of a live-data prototype.

A *live-data prototype* is a very limited implementation. It typically has none of the productization that's normally required, such as the full set of use cases, automated tests, full analytics instrumentation, internationalization and localization, performance and scalability, SEO work, and so forth.

The live-data prototype is substantially smaller than the eventual product, and the bar is dramatically lower in terms of quality, performance, and functionality. It needs to run well enough to collect data for some very specific use cases, and that's about it.

When creating a live-data prototype, our engineers don't handle all the use cases. They don't address internationalization and localization work, they don't tackle performance or scalability, they don't create the automated tests, and they only include instrumentation for the specific use cases we're testing.

> *The key is to be able to send some limited amount of traffic, and to collect analytics on how this live-data prototype is being used.*

A live-data prototype is just a small fraction of the productization effort (in my experience, somewhere between 5 and 10 percent of the eventual delivery productization work), but you get big value from it. There are two big limitations you do have to keep in mind, however:

- First, this is code, so engineers must create the live-data prototype, not your designers.

- Second, this is not a commercially shippable product, it's not ready for primetime, and you can't run a business on it. So, if the live-data tests go well, and you decide to move forward and productize, you will need to allow your engineers to take the time required to do the necessary delivery work. It is definitely *not* okay for the product manager to tell the engineers that this is "good enough." That judgment is not up to the product manager. And the product manager does need to make sure key executives and stakeholders understand the limitations as well.

Today, the technology for creating live-data prototypes is so good that we can often get what we need in just a couple days to a week. And once we have it we can iterate very quickly.

Later, we'll discuss the quantitative-validation techniques and you'll see the different ways we can utilize this live-data prototype. But for now, know that the key is to be able to send some limited amount of traffic, and to collect analytics on how this live-data prototype is being used.

What's important is that actual users will use the live-data prototype for real work, and this will generate real data (analytics) that we can compare to our current product—or to our expectations—to see if this new approach performs better.

Hybrid Prototype Technique

So far, we've explored user prototypes—which are pure simulations—feasibility prototypes for addressing technical risks, and live-data prototypes designed to be able to collect evidence, or even statistically significant proof, as to the effectiveness of a product or an idea.

While these three categories of prototypes handle most situations well, a wide variety of hybrid prototypes also combine different aspects of each of these in different ways.

One of my favorite examples of a hybrid prototype—and an exceptionally powerful tool for learning quickly in product discovery—is today often referred to as a *Wizard of Oz* prototype. A Wizard of Oz prototype combines the front-end user experience of a high-fidelity user prototype but with an actual person behind the scenes performing manually what would ultimately be handled by automation.

A Wizard of Oz prototype is *absolutely* not scalable, and we would never send any significant amount of traffic to this. But the benefit from our perspective is that we can create this very quickly and easily, and from the user's perspective, it looks and behaves like a real product.

For example, imagine that today you have some sort of live chat–based help for your customers, but it's only available during the hours when your customer service staff is in the office. You know that your customers use your product

> *These types of hybrids are great examples of the* build things that don't scale *philosophy of product discovery.*

from all around the world at all hours, so you would like to develop an automated chat-based system that provides helpful answers anytime.

You could (and should) talk to your customer service staff about the types of inquiries they routinely get and how they respond (a *concierge test* could help you learn that quickly). Soon you will want to tackle the challenges of this sort of automation.

One way to learn very quickly and test out several different approaches is to create a Wizard of Oz prototype that provides a simple, chat-based interface. However, behind the scenes it is literally you as product manager, or another member of your team, who is receiving the requests and composing responses. Soon we begin to experiment with system-generated responses, perhaps even using a live-data prototype of our algorithm.

These types of hybrids are great examples of the *build things that don't scale* philosophy of product discovery. By being a little clever, we can quickly and easily create tools that let us learn very quickly. Admittedly, it's mainly qualitative learning, but that's often where our biggest insights come from anyway.

Discovery Testing Techniques

Overview

In product discovery, we're essentially trying to quickly separate the good ideas from the bad as we work to try to solve the business problems assigned to us. But what does that really mean?

We think of four types of questions we're trying to answer during discovery:

1. Will the user or customer choose to use or buy this? (Value)
2. Can the user figure out how to use this? (Usability)
3. Can we build this? (Feasibility)
4. Is this solution viable for our business? (Business viability)

Remember that for many of the things we work on, most or all of these questions are very straightforward and low risk. Your team is confident. They have been there and done this many times before, and so we will proceed to delivery.

The main activity of discovery is when these answers are not so clear.

There is no prescribed order to answering these questions. However, many teams follow a certain logic.

First, we will usually assess value. This is often the toughest—and most important—question to answer, and if the value isn't there, not much else matters. We likely will need to address usability before

the user or customer can even recognize the value. In either case, we
usually assess usability and value
with the same users and customers
at the same time.

> *In product discovery, we're
> essentially trying to quickly
> separate the good ideas from
> the bad as we work to try to
> solve the business problems
> assigned to us.*

Once we have something
that our customers believe is truly
valuable, and we have designed it in
a way that we believe our users can figure out how to use, then we'll
typically review the approach with the engineers to make sure this is
doable from their technical feasibility perspective.

If we're also good on feasibility, then we'll show it to key parts
of the business where there may be concerns (think legal, marketing,
sales, CEO, etc.). We'll often address these business risks last because
we don't want to stir up the organization unless we're confident it's
worthwhile. Also, sometimes the ideas that survive are not so similar
to the original ideas that we started with, and those original ideas may
have come from a business stakeholder. It's much more effective to be
able to show that stakeholder some evidence of what did and didn't
work with customers and why and how you ended up where you are.

50

Testing Usability

U sability testing is typically the most mature and straightforward form of discovery testing, and it has existed for many years. The tools are better and teams do much more of this now than they used to, and this is not rocket science. The main difference today is that we do usability testing in discovery—using prototypes, before we build the product—and not at the end, where it's really too late to correct the issues without significant waste or worse.

If your company is large enough to have its own user research group, by all means secure as much of their time for your team as you absolutely can. Even if you can't get much of their time, these people are often terrific resources, and if you can make a friend in this group, it can be a huge help to you.

If your organization has funds earmarked for outside services, you may be able to use one of many user research firms to conduct the testing for you. But at the price that most firms charge, chances are that you won't be able to afford nearly as much of this type of testing as your product will need. If you're like most companies, you have few resources available, and even less money. But you can't let that stop you.

So, I'll show you how to do this testing yourself.

No, you won't be as proficient as a trained user researcher—at least at first—and it'll take you a few sessions to get the hang of it, but, in most cases, you'll find that you can still identify the serious issues and friction points with your product, which is what's important.

There are several excellent books that describe how to conduct informal usability testing, so I won't try to recreate those here. Instead, I'll just emphasize the key points.

Recruiting Users to Test

You'll need to round up some test subjects. If you're using a user research group, they'll likely recruit and schedule the users for you, which is a huge help, but if you're on your own, you've got several options:

- If you've established the customer-discovery program I described earlier, you are probably all set—at least if you're building a product for businesses. If you're working on a consumer product, you'll want to supplement that group.

- You can advertise for test subjects on Craigslist, or you can set up an SEM campaign using Google AdWords to recruit users (which is especially good if you are looking for users that are *in the moment* of trying to use a product like yours).

- If you have a list of e-mail addresses of your users, you can do a selection from there. Your product marketing manager often can help you narrow down the list.

- You can solicit volunteers on your company website—lots of major companies do this now. Remember that you'll still call and screen the volunteers to make sure the people you select are in your target market.

- You can always go to where your users congregate. Trade shows for business software, shopping centers for e-commerce, sports bars for fantasy sports—you get the idea. If your product is addressing a real need, you usually won't have trouble getting people to give you an hour. Bring some thank-you gifts.

- If you're asking users to come to your location, you will likely need to compensate them for their time. We often will arrange to meet the test subject at a mutually convenient location, such as a Starbucks. This practice is so common it's usually referred to as *Starbucks testing*.

Preparing the Test

- We usually do usability testing with a *high-fidelity user prototype*. You can get some useful usability feedback with a low- or medium-fidelity user prototype, but for the value testing that typically follows usability testing, we need the product to be more realistic (more on why later).

- Most of the time, when we do a usability and/or value test, it's with the product manager, the product designer, and one of the engineers from the team (from those that like to attend these). I like to rotate among the engineers. As I mentioned earlier, the magic often happens when an engineer is present, so I try to encourage that whenever possible. If you have a user researcher helping with the actual testing, they will typically administer the test, but absolutely the product manager and designer must be there for each and every test.

- You will need to define in advance the set of tasks that you want to test. Usually, these are fairly obvious. If, for example, you're building an alarm clock app for a mobile device, your users will need to do things like set an alarm, find and hit the snooze button, and so on. There may also be more obscure tasks, but concentrate on the primary tasks—the ones that users will do most of the time.

- Some people still believe that the product manager and the product designer are too close to the product to do this type of testing objectively, and they may either get their feelings hurt or only hear what they want to hear. We get past this obstacle in two ways. First, we train the product managers and designers on how to conduct themselves, and second, we make sure the test happens quickly—before they fall in love with their own ideas. Good product managers know they will get the product wrong initially and that nobody gets it right the first time. They know that learning from these tests is the fastest path to a successful product.

- You should have one person administer the usability test and another person taking notes. It's helpful to have at least one other person to debrief with afterward to make sure you both saw the same things and came to the same conclusions.

- Formal testing labs will typically have setups with two-way mirrors or closed-circuit video monitors with cameras that capture both the screen and the user from the front. This is fine if you have it, but I can't count how many prototypes I've tested at a tiny table at Starbucks—just big enough for three or four chairs around the table. In fact, in many ways, this is preferable to the testing lab because the user feels a lot less like a lab rat.

- The other environment that works really well is your customer's office. It can be time consuming to do, but even 30 minutes in their office can tell you a lot. They are masters of their domain and often very talkative. In addition, all the cues are there to remind them of how they might use the product. You can also learn from seeing what their office looks like. How big is their monitor? How fast is their computer and network connectivity? How do they communicate with their colleagues on their work tasks?

- There are tools for doing this type of testing remotely, and I encourage that, but they are primarily designed for usability testing and not for the value testing that will usually follow. So, I view the remote usability testing as a supplement rather than a replacement.

Testing Your Prototype

Now that you've got your prototype ready, lined up your test subjects, and prepared the tasks and questions, here are a set of tips and techniques for administering the actual test.

Before you jump in, we want to take the opportunity to learn how they think about this problem today. If you remember the key questions from the *Customer Interview Technique*, we want to learn whether the user or customer really has

> *We want to learn whether the user or customer really has the problems we think they have, and how they solve those problems today, and what it would take for them to switch.*

the problems we think they have, and how they solve those problems today, and what it would take for them to switch.

- When you first start the actual usability test, make sure to tell your subject that this is just a prototype, it's a very early product idea, and it's not real. Explain that she won't be hurting your feelings by giving her candid feedback, good or bad. You're testing the ideas in the prototype, you're not testing *her*. *She* can't pass or fail—only the prototype can pass or fail.

- One more thing before you jump into your tasks: See if they can tell from the landing page of your prototype what it is that you do, and especially what might be valuable or appealing to them. Again, once they jump into tasks, you'll lose that first-time visitor context, so don't waste the opportunity. You'll find that landing pages are incredibly important to bridging the gap between expectations and what the product does.

- When testing, you'll want to do everything you can to keep your users in *use mode* and out of *critique mode*. What matters is whether users can easily do the tasks they need to do. It really doesn't matter if the user thinks something on the page is ugly or should be moved or changed. Sometimes misguided testers will ask users questions like "What three things on the page would you change?" To me, unless that user happens to be a product designer, I'm not really interested in that. If users knew what they really wanted, software would be a lot easier to create. So, watch what they do more than what they say.

- During the testing, the main skill you have to learn is to keep quiet. When we see someone struggle, most of us have a natural urge to help the person out. You need to suppress that urge. It's your job to turn into a horrible conversationalist. Get comfortable with silence—it's your friend.

- There are three important cases you're looking for: (1) the user got through the task with no problem at all and no help; (2) the user struggled and moaned a bit, but he eventually got through it; or (3) he got so frustrated he gave up. Sometimes people will give up quickly, so you may need to encourage them to keep trying a bit longer. But, if he gets to the point that you believe he would truly leave the product and go to a competitor, then that's when you note that he truly gave up.

- In general, you'll want to avoid giving any help or *leading the witness* in any way. If you see the user scrolling the page up and down and clearly looking for something, it's okay to ask the user what specifically she's looking for, as that information is very valuable to you. Some people ask users to keep a running narration of what they're thinking, but I find this tends to put people in critique mode, as it's not a natural behavior.

- Act like a parrot. This helps in many ways. First, it helps avoid leading. If they're quiet and you really can't stand it because you're uncomfortable, tell them what they're doing: "I see that you're looking at the list on the right." This will prompt them to tell you what they're trying to do, what they're looking for, or whatever it may be. If they ask a question, rather than giving a leading answer, you can play back the question to them. They ask, "Will clicking on this make a new entry?" and you ask in return, "You're wondering if clicking on this will make a new entry?" Usually, they will take it from there because they'll want to answer your question: "Yeah, I think it will." Parroting also helps avoid leading value judgments. If you have the urge to say, "Great!" instead you can say, "You created a new entry." Finally, parroting key points also helps your note taker because she has more time to write down important things.

- Fundamentally, you're trying to get an understanding of how your target users think about this problem and to identify places in your prototype where the model the software presents is inconsistent or incompatible with how the user is thinking about the problem. That's what it means to be counterintuitive. Fortunately, when you spot this, it is not usually hard to fix, and it can be a big win for your product.

- You will find that you can tell a great deal from body language and tone. It's painfully obvious when they don't like your ideas, and it's also clear when they genuinely do. They'll almost always ask for an e-mail when the product is out if they like what they see. And, if they really like it, they'll try to get it early from you.

Summarizing the Learning

The point is to gain a deeper understanding of your users and customers and, of course, to identify the friction points in the prototype so you can fix them. It might be nomenclature, flow, visual design issues, or mental model issues, but as soon as you think you've identified an issue, just fix it in the prototype. There's no law that says you have to keep the test identical for all of your test subjects. That kind of thinking stems from misunderstanding the role this type of qualitative testing plays. We're not trying to prove anything here; we're just trying to learn quickly.

After each test subject, or after each set of tests, someone—usually either the product manager or the designer—writes up a short summary e-mail of key learnings and sends it out to the product team. But forget big reports that take a long time to write, are seldom read, and are obsolete by the time they're delivered because the prototype has already progressed so far beyond what was used when the tests were done. They really aren't worth anyone's time.

> *The point is to gain a deeper understanding of your users and customers and, of course, to identify the friction points in the prototype so you can fix them.*

CHAPTER
51

Testing Value

Customers don't have to buy our products, and users don't have to choose to use a feature. They will only do so if they perceive real *value*. Another way to think about this is that just because someone *can* use our product doesn't mean they will *choose* to use our product. This is especially true when you are trying to get your customers or users to switch from whatever product or system they were using before to your new product. And, most of the time, our users and customers are switching from something—even if that something is a homegrown solution.

So many companies and product teams think all they need to do is match the features (referred to as *feature parity*), and then they don't understand why their product doesn't sell, even at a lower price.

The customer must perceive your product to be *substantially better* to motivate them to buy your product and then wade through the pain and obstacles of migrating from their old solution.

All of this is a long way of saying that good product teams spend most of their time on creating value. If the value is there, we can fix everything else. If it's not, how good our usability, reliability, or performance is doesn't matter.

There are several elements of value, and there are techniques for testing all of them.

> *Just because someone can use our product doesn't mean they will choose to use our product.*

Testing Demand

Sometimes it's unclear if there's *demand* for what we want to build. In other words, if we could come up with an amazing solution to this problem, do customers even care about this problem? Enough to buy a new product and switch to it? This concept of demand testing applies to entire products, down to a specific feature on an existing product.

We can't just assume there's demand, although often the demand is well established because most of the time our products are entering an existing market with demonstrated and measurable demand. The real challenge in that situation is whether we can come up with a demonstrably better solution in terms of value than the alternatives.

Testing Value Qualitatively

The most common type of qualitative value testing is focused on the *response*, or reaction. Do customers love this? Will they pay for it? Will users choose to use this? And most important, if not, why not?

Testing Value Quantitatively

For many products, we need to test *efficacy*, which refers to how well this solution solves the underlying problem. In some types of products, this is very objective and quantitative. For example, in advertising technology, we can measure the revenue generated and easily compare that to other advertising technology alternatives. In other types of products, such as games, it's much less objective.

52

Demand Testing Techniques

One of the biggest possible wastes of time and effort, and the reason for countless failed startups, is when a team designs and builds a product—testing usability, testing reliability, testing performance, and doing everything they think they're supposed to do—yet, when they finally release the product, they find that people won't buy it.

Even worse, it's not like they sign up for a trial in significant numbers, but then for some reason don't decide to buy. We can usually recover from that. It's that they don't even want to sign up for the trial. That's a tremendous and often fatal problem.

You might experiment with pricing, positioning, and marketing, but you eventually conclude that this is just not a problem people are concerned enough about.

The worst part of this scenario is that, in my experience, it's so easily avoided.

The problem I just described can happen at the product level, such as an all-new product from a startup, or at the feature level. The feature example is depressingly common. Every day, new features get deployed that don't get used. And, this case is even easier to prevent.

Suppose you were contemplating a new feature, perhaps because a large customer is asking for it or maybe because you saw that a competitor has the feature or maybe it's your CEO's pet feature. You talk about the feature with your team, and your engineers point out to you that the implementation cost is substantial. Not impossible but not easy either—enough that you don't want to take the time to build this only to find out later it wasn't used.

> *One of the biggest possible wastes of time and effort, and the reason for countless failed startups, is when a team designs and builds a product, yet, when they finally release the product, they find that people won't buy it.*

The demand-testing technique is called a *fake door demand test*. The idea is that we put the button or menu item into the user experience exactly where we believe it should be. But, when the user clicks that button, rather than taking the user to the new feature, it instead takes the user to a special page that explains that you are studying the possibility of adding this new feature, and you are seeking customers to talk to about this. The page also provides a way for the user to volunteer (by providing their e-mail or phone number, for example).

What's critical for this to be effective is that the users not have any visible indication that this is a test until after they click that button. The benefit is that we can quickly collect some very helpful data that will allow us to compare the click-through rate on this button with our expectations or with other features. And then we can follow up with customers to get a better understanding of what they would expect.

The same basic concept applies to entire products. Rather than a button on a page, we set up the landing page for the new offering's product funnel. This is called a *landing page demand test*. We describe that new offering exactly as we would if we were really launching the service. The difference is that if the user clicks the call to action, rather than signing up for the trial (or whatever the action might be), the user sees a page that explains that you are studying the possibility of adding this new offering, and you'd like to talk with them about that new offering if they're willing.

With both forms of demand testing, we can show the test to every user (in the case of an early startup) or we can show it to just a very small percentage of users or within in a specific geography (in the case of a larger company).

Hopefully, you can see that this is very easy to do, and you can quickly collect two very useful things: (1) some good evidence on demand and (2) a list of users who are very ready and willing to talk with you about this specific new capability.

In practice, the demand is usually not the problem. People do sign up for our trial. The problem is that they try out our product and they don't get excited about it—at least not excited enough to switch from what they currently use. And dealing with that is the purpose of the qualitative and quantitative techniques in the chapters that follow.

Discovery Testing in Risk-Averse Companies

Much has been written about how to do product discovery in startups—by me and by many others. There are many challenges for startups, but most important is survival.

One of the real advantages to startups from a product point of view is that there's no legacy to drag along, no revenue to preserve, and no reputation to safeguard. This allows us to move very quickly and take significant risks without much downside.

However, once your product develops to the point that it can sustain a viable business (congratulations!), you now have something to lose, and it's not surprising that some of the dynamics of product discovery need to change. My goal here is to highlight these differences and to describe how the techniques are modified in larger, enterprise companies.

Others have also been writing about how to apply these techniques in enterprises, but on the whole, I have not been particularly impressed with the advice I've seen. Too often, the suggestion is to carve out a protected team and provide them some air cover so they can go off and innovate. First of all, what does this say about the people not on these *special* innovation teams? What does this say

(continued)

(continued)

about the company's *existing* products? And, even when something does get some traction, how well do you think the existing product teams will accept this learning? These

> *The most important point for technology companies: If you stop innovating, you will die.*

are some of the reasons I'm not an advocate of so-called corporate innovation labs.

I have long argued that the techniques of product discovery and rapid test and learn absolutely apply to large enterprise companies, and not just to startups. The best product companies—including Apple, Amazon, Google, Facebook, and Netflix—are great examples where this kind of innovation is institutionalized. In these companies, innovation is not something that just a few people get permission to pursue. It is the responsibility of *all* product teams.

But before I go any further, I want to emphasize the most important point for technology companies: If you stop innovating, you will die. Maybe not immediately, but if all you do is optimize your existing solutions, and you stop innovating, it is only a matter of time before you are someone else's lunch.

> *That said, we need to do this in a responsible way.*

I believe it's a non-negotiable that we simply must continue to move our products forward, and deliver increased value to our customers.

That said, we need to do this in a responsible way. This really means doing two really big things—protect your revenue and brand, and protect your employees and customers.

Protect Revenue and Brand

The company has built a reputation and has earned revenue, and it is the job of the product teams to do product discovery in ways that protect this reputation and this revenue. We've got more techniques than ever to do this, including many techniques for creating very low-cost

(continued)

(continued)

and low-risk prototypes, and for proving things work with minimal investment and limited exposure. We love live-data prototypes and A/B testing frameworks.

Many things do not pose a risk to brand or revenue, but for the things that do, we utilize techniques to mitigate this risk. Most of the time an A/B test with 1 percent or less of the customers exposed is fine for this.

Sometimes, however, we need to be even more conservative. In such cases, we'll do an invite-only live-data test, or we'll utilize our customer discovery program customers that are under NDA. There are any number of other techniques in the same spirit of test and learn in a responsible way.

Protect Employees and Customers

In addition to protecting revenue and brand, we also need to protect our employees and our customers. If our customer service, professional services, or sales staff are blindsided by constant change, it makes it very hard for them to do their jobs and take good care of customers.

Similarly, customers that feel like your product is a moving target that they have to constantly relearn won't be happy customers for long.

This is why we use gentle deployment techniques, including assessing customer impact. Although this may seem counterintuitive, continuous deployment is a very powerful gentle deployment technique, and when used properly along with customer impact assessment, it is a powerful tool for protecting our customers.

Again, most experiments and changes are non-issues, but it is our responsibility to be proactive with customers and employees and sensitive to change.

Don't get me wrong. I am not arguing that innovating in enterprise companies is easy—it's not. But it's not because product discovery techniques are the obstacles to innovation. They are absolutely critical to consistently delivering increased value to customers.

(continued)

(continued)

There are broader issues in large enterprise companies that typically create obstacles to innovation.

If you are at a larger, enterprise company, know that you absolutely must move aggressively to continuously improve your product, well beyond small optimizations. But you also must do this product work in ways that protect brand and revenue, and protect your employees and your customers.

53

Qualitative Value Testing Techniques

Quantitative testing tells us what's happening (or not), but it can't tell us *why*, and what to do to correct the situation. That's why we do qualitative testing. If users and customers are not responding to a product the way we had hoped, we need to figure out why that's the case.

As a reminder, qualitative testing is not about proving anything. That's what quantitative testing is for. Qualitative testing is about rapid learning and big insights.

When you do this type of qualitative user testing, you don't get your answer from any one user, but every user you test with is like another piece of the puzzle. Eventually, you see enough of the puzzle that you can understand where you've gone wrong.

> *I argue that qualitative testing of your product ideas with real users and customers is probably* the single most important discovery activity *for you and your product team.*

I know this is a big claim, but I argue that qualitative testing of your product ideas with real users and customers is probably *the single most important discovery activity* for you and your product team. It is so important and helpful that I push product teams to do at least *two or three qualitative value tests every single week*. Here's how to do it:

Interview First

We generally begin the user test with a short user interview where we try to make sure our user has the problems we think she has, how she solves these problems today, and what it would take for her to switch (see Customer Interview Technique).

Usability Test

We have many good techniques for testing value qualitatively, but they all depend on the user first understanding what your product is and how it works. This is why a value test is always preceded by a usability test.

During the usability test, we test to see whether the user can figure out how to operate our product. But, even more important, after a usability test the user knows what your product is all about and how it's meant to be used. Only then can we have a useful conversation with the user about value (or lack thereof).

Preparing a value test therefore includes preparing a usability test. I described how to prepare for and run a usability test in the last chapter, so for now let me again emphasize that it's important to conduct the usability test *before* the value test, and to do one immediately after the other.

If you try to do a value test without giving the user or customer the opportunity to learn how to use the product, then the value test becomes more like a focus group where people talk hypothetically about your product, and try to imagine how it might work. To be clear: focus groups might be helpful for gaining market insights, but they are not helpful in discovering the product we need to deliver (see Product Discovery Principle #1).

This testing involves at least you as product manager and your product designer, but I am constantly amazed at how often the *magic* happens when one of your engineers is right there watching the qualitative testing with you. So, it's worth your pushing to make this happen as much as possible.

To test usability and value, the user needs to be able to use one of the prototypes we described earlier. When we're focused on testing value, we usually utilize *high-fidelity user prototypes*.

High-fidelity means it feels very realistic, which turns out to be especially important for value testing. You can also use a live-data prototype or a hybrid prototype.

Specific Value Tests

The main challenge in testing value when you're sitting face to face with actual users and customers is that people are generally nice—and not willing to tell you what they *really* think. So, all of our tests for value are designed to make sure the person is *not just being nice to you*.

Using Money to Demonstrate Value

One technique I like for gauging value is to see if the user would be willing to pay for it, even if you have no intention of charging them for it. We're looking for the user to pull out his or her credit card right then and there and ask to buy the product (but we don't really want the card information).

If it's an expensive product for businesses—beyond what someone would put on a credit card—you can ask people if they will sign a "non-binding letter of intent to buy" which is a good indicator that people are serious.

Using Reputation to Demonstrate Value

But there are other ways a user can "pay" for a product. You can see if they would be willing to pay with their reputation. You can ask them how likely they'd be to recommend the product to their friends or co-workers or boss (typically on a scale of 0–10). You can ask them to share on social media. You can ask them to enter the e-mail of their boss or their friends for a recommendation (even though we don't save the e-mails, it's very meaningful if people are willing to provide them).

Using Time to Demonstrate Value

Especially with businesses, you can also ask the person if they'd be willing to schedule some significant time with you to work on this (even if we don't need it). This is another way people pay for value.

Using Access to Demonstrate Value

You can also ask people to provide the login credentials for whatever product they would be switching from (because you tell them there's a migration utility or something). Again, we don't really want their login and password—we just want to know if they value our product highly enough that they're truly willing to switch right then and there.

Iterating the Prototype

Remember, this is not about proving anything. It's about rapid learning. As soon as you believe you have a problem, or you want to try a different approach, you try it.

For example, if you show your prototype to two different people and the response you get is substantially different, your job is to try to figure out why. Maybe you have two different types of customers, with different kinds of problems. Maybe you have different types of users, with different skill sets or domain knowledge. Maybe they are running different solutions today, and one is happy with their current solution and one is not.

You might determine that you just aren't able to get people interested in this problem, or you can't figure out a way to make this usable enough that your target users can realize this value. In that case, you may decide to stop right there and put the idea on the shelf. Some product managers consider this a big failure. I view it as saving the company

the wasted cost of building and
shipping a product your customers
don't value (and won't buy), plus
the opportunity cost of what your
engineering team could be building
instead.

> *As product manager, you need to make sure you are at every single qualitative value test. Do not delegate this.*

The remarkable thing about
this kind of qualitative testing is just how easy and effective it is. The
best way to prove this to yourself is to take your laptop or mobile device
with your product or prototype on it to someone who hasn't seen it yet,
and just give it a try.

One important note. As product manager, you need to make sure
you are at every single qualitative value test. Do not delegate this, and
certainly don't try to hire a firm to do this for you. Your contribution to
the team comes from experiencing as many users as possible, first hand,
interacting with and responding to your team's ideas. If you worked for
me, the continuation of your monthly salary would depend on this.

54

Quantitative Value Testing Techniques

While qualitative testing is all about fast learning and big insights, quantitative techniques are all about collecting evidence.

We will sometimes collect enough data that we have *statistically significant results* (especially with consumer services with a lot of daily traffic), and other times we'll set the bar lower and just collect actual usage data that we consider useful *evidence*—along with other factors—to make an informed decision.

This is the main purpose of the live-data prototype we discussed earlier. As a reminder, a live-data prototype is one of the forms of prototype created in product discovery intended to expose certain use cases to a limited group of users to collect some actual usage data.

We have a few key ways to collect this data, and the technique we select depends on the amount of traffic we have, the amount of time we have, and our tolerance for risk.

In a true startup environment, we don't have much traffic and we also don't have much time, but we're usually fine with risk (we don't have much to lose yet).

> *While qualitative testing is all about fast learning and big insights, quantitative techniques are all about collecting evidence.*

In a more established company, we often have a lot of traffic, we have some amount of time (mostly we're worried about management losing patience), and the company is usually more averse to risk.

A/B Testing

The gold standard for this type of testing is an A/B test. The reason we love A/B tests is because the user doesn't know which version of the product she is seeing. This yields data that is very predictive, which is what we ideally want.

Keep in mind that this is a slightly different type of A/B test than *optimization A/B testing*. Optimization testing is where we experiment with different calls to action, different color treatments on a button, and so forth. Conceptually they are the same, but in practice there are some differences. Optimization testing is normally surface-level, low-risk changes, which we often test in a split test (50:50).

In *discovery A/B testing*, we usually have the current product showing to 99 percent of our users, and the live-data prototype showing to only 1 percent of our users or less. We monitor the A/B test more closely.

Invite-Only Testing

If your company is more risk averse, or if you just don't have enough traffic to be able to show to 1 percent—or even 10 percent—and get useful results anytime soon, then another effective way to collect evidence is the *invite-only* test. This is where you identify a set of users or customers that you contact and invite to try the new version. You tell them that it is an experimental version, so they are effectively opting in if they choose to run it.

The data that this group generates is not as predictive as from a true, blind, A/B test. We realize that those who opt in are generally more early adopter types; nevertheless, we are getting a set of actual users doing their work with our live-data prototype, and we are collecting really interesting data.

I can't tell you how often we think we have something they'll love, and then we make it available to a limited group like this and we find that they are just not feeling it. Unfortunately, with a quantitative test like this all we know for sure is that they're not using it—we can't know why. That's when we'll follow up with a qualitative test to try and quickly learn why they're not as into it as we had hoped.

Customer Discovery Program

A variation of the invite-only test is to use the members of the customer discovery program we discussed in the section on ideation techniques. These companies have already opted in to testing new versions, and you already have a close relationship with them so you can follow up with them easily.

For products for businesses, I typically use this as my primary technique for collecting actual usage data. We have the customer discovery program customers getting frequent updates to the live-data prototype, and we compare their usage data to that of our broader customers.

The Role of Analytics

One of the most significant changes in how we do product today is our use of analytics. Any capable product manager today is expected to be comfortable with data and understand how to leverage analytics to learn and improve quickly.

I attribute this change to several factors.

First, as the market for our products has expanded dramatically due to access globally—and also by way of connected devices—the

(continued)

(continued)

sheer volume of data has
dramatically increased, which
gives us interesting and statistically significantly results
much faster.

> *Any capable product
> manager today is expected
> to be comfortable with data
> and understand how to
> leverage analytics to learn
> and improve quickly.*

Second, the tools for
accessing and learning from
this data have improved signif-
icantly. Mostly, however, I see an increased awareness of the role that
data can play in helping you learn and adapt quickly.

There are five main uses of analytics in strong product teams.
Let's take a close look at each of these uses:

Understand User and Customer Behavior

When most people think of analytics, they think of *user* analytics. That
is, however, but one type of analytic. The idea is to understand how
our users and customers are using our products (remember, there can
be many users at a single customer—at least in the B2B context). We
may do this to identify features that are not being used, or to confirm
that features are being used as we expect, or simply to gain a better
understanding of the difference between what people say and what
they actually do.

This type of analytic has been collected and used for this purpose by good product teams for at least 30 years. A solid decade before
the emergence of the web, desktops and servers were able to call home
and upload behavior analytics, which were then used by the product team to make improvements. This to me is one of the very few
non-negotiables in product. My view is that, if you're going to put a
feature in, you need to put in at least the basic usage analytics for that
feature. Otherwise, how will you know if it's working as it needs to?

Measure Product Progress

I have long been a strong advocate of using data to drive product
teams. Rather than provide the team an old-style roadmap listing
(continued)

(continued)

someone's best guess of what features may or may not work, I strongly prefer to provide the product team with a set of business objectives—with measurable goals—and then the team makes the calls as to what are the best ways to achieve those goals. It's part of the larger trend in product to focus on outcome and not output.

Prove Whether Product Ideas Work

Today, especially for consumer companies, we can isolate the contribution of new features, new versions of workflows, or new designs by running A/B tests and then comparing the results. This lets us prove which of our ideas work. We don't have to do this with everything, but with things that have high risk or high deployment costs, or that require changes in user behavior, this can be a tremendously powerful tool. Even where the volume of traffic is such that collecting statistically significant results is difficult or time consuming, we can still collect actual data from our live-data prototypes to make decisions that are much better informed.

Inform Product Decisions

In my experience, the worst thing about product in the past was its reliance on opinions. And, usually, the higher up in the organization the person was who voiced it, the more that opinion counted.

Today, in the spirit of *data beats opinions*, we have the option of simply running a test, collecting some data, and then using that data to inform our decisions. The data is not everything, and we are not slaves to it, but I find countless examples today in the best product teams of decisions informed by test results. I hear constantly from teams how often they are surprised by the data, and how minds are changed by it.

Inspire Product Work

While I am personally hooked on each of the above roles of analytics, I must admit that my personal favorite is this last point. The data we

(continued)

(continued)

aggregate (from all sources) can be a gold mine. It often boils down to asking the right questions. But by exploring the data, we can find some very powerful product opportunities. Some of the best product work I see going on right now was inspired by the data. Yes, we often get great ideas by observing our customers, and we do often get great ideas by applying new technology. But studying the data itself can provide insights that lead to breakthrough product ideas.

Largely, this is because the data often catches us off guard. We have a set of assumptions about how the product is used—most of which we are not even conscious of—and when we see the data, we're surprised that it doesn't track with those assumptions. It's these surprises that lead to real progress.

It's also important for tech product managers to have a broad understanding of the types of analytics that are important to your product. Many have too narrow of a view. Here is the core set for most tech products:

- User behavior analytics (click paths, engagement)
- Business analytics (active users, conversion rate, lifetime value, retention)
- Financial analytics (ASP, billings, time to close)
- Performance (load time, uptime)
- Operational costs (storage, hosting)
- Go-to-market costs (acquisition costs, cost of sales, programs)
- Sentiment (NPS, customer satisfaction, surveys)

Hopefully, you can see the power of analytics for product teams. However, as powerful as the role of data is for us, the most important thing to keep in mind about analytics is that the data will shine a light on *what* is happening, but it won't explain *why*. We need our qualitative techniques to explain the quantitative results.

Note that we often refer to analytics as *key performance indicators* (KPIs).

Flying Blind

Remarkably, I still encounter too many product teams that either aren't instrumenting their product to collect analytics, or they do it at such a minor level that they don't know if and how their product is being used.

My own teams—and every team I can think of that I've ever worked with—have been doing this for so long now that it's hard to imagine not having this information. It's hard for me to even remember what it was like to have no real idea how the product was used, or what features were really helping the customer, versus which ones we thought had to be there just to help close a sale.

This is easiest to do with cloud-based products and services, and most of us use web analytics tools, but sometimes we use homegrown tools for this too.

Good product teams have been doing this for years. And, not just with cloud-based sites, but also with installed mobile or desktop applications—on-premise software, hardware, and devices that call home periodically and send the usage data back to the teams. A few companies are very conservative and ask permission before sending the data, but mostly this just happens silently.

We should all be anonymizing and aggregating the data so there's nothing personally identifiable in there. Occasionally, however, we see in the news that another company is in trouble for sending raw data in the rush to market. It seems the press thinks we're tracking these data for nefarious purposes, but at least with the companies I know and work with, they're simply trying to make the products better—more valuable and more usable. This has long been one of our most important tools for doing so.

The way the overall process works is that we first ask ourselves what we need to know about how our products are used, then we

(continued)

(continued)

instrument the product to collect this information (the particular techniques depend on
the tool you're using and what
you want to collect). Finally,
we generate various forms of
online reports to view and
interpret these data.

> *I still encounter too many product teams that either aren't instrumenting their product to collect analytics, or they do it at such a minor level that they don't know if and how their product is being used.*

For everything new we
add, we ensure we have the
necessary instrumentation in
place to know immediately if it is working as we expect, and if there
are significant unintended consequences. Frankly, without that instrumentation, I wouldn't bother to roll out the feature. How would you
know if it was working?

For most product managers, the first thing they do in the
morning is to check the analytics to see what happened during the
preceding night. They're usually running some form of test almost
all the time, so they're very interested in what's happened.

There are of course some extreme environments where
everything lives behind very strict firewalls, but even then, the
products can generate periodic usage reports to be reviewed and
approved before being forwarded (via electronic or printed reports,
if necessary) back to the teams.

I'm very big on radically simplifying products by removing
features that don't carry their own weight. But, without knowing
what is being used, and how it's being used, it's a very painful process
to do this when you don't know what's really going on. We don't
have the data to back up our theories or decisions, so management
(rightfully) balks.

My personal view is that you should start from the position that
you simply must have this data, and then work backward from there
to figure out the best way to get it.

55

Testing Feasibility

W hen we talk about validating feasibility, the engineers are really trying to answer several related questions:

- Do we know *how* to build this?
- Do we have the *skills* on the team to build this?
- Do we have enough *time* to build this?
- Do we need any *architectural* changes to build this?
- Do we have on hand all the *components* we need to build this?
- Do we understand the *dependencies* involved in building this?
- Will the *performance* be acceptable?
- Will it *scale* to the levels we need?
- Do we have the *infrastructure* necessary to test and run this?
- Can we afford the *cost* to provision this?

I don't want to scare you. With most product ideas that your engineers review in discovery, they will quickly consider these points and simply say "No problem." That's because most of our work is not all that new, and engineers have usually built similar things many times before.

However, there are definitely ideas where this is not the case, and some or many of these questions can be very difficult for the engineers to answer.

One very common example right now is that many teams are evaluating machine-learning technology, considering build/buy decisions, and assessing whether the technology is suitable for the job at hand—and, more generally, trying to understand its potential.

Here's some very practical and important advice for you to consider. Holding a weekly planning meeting where you throw a bunch of ideas at the engineers—and demand they give you some sort of estimate either in time, story points, or any other unit of effort—is almost certain to go badly. If you put an engineer on the spot, without time to investigate and consider, you are very likely to get a conservative answer, partly designed to make you go away.

If, however, the engineers have been following along as the team has tried out these ideas with customers (using prototypes) and seen what the issues are and how people feel about these ideas, the engineers have probably already been considering the issues for some time. If it's something you think is worthwhile, then you need to give the engineers some time to investigate and consider it.

The question isn't, "Can you do this?" Rather, you are asking them to look into it and answer the question, "What's the best way to do this and how long would it take?"

The engineers will sometimes come back and say they need to create a *feasibility prototype* to answer one or more of these questions. If that's the case, first consider whether the idea is potentially worth investing the necessary time in discovery. If so, then encourage the engineers to proceed.

One last point on assessing feasibility: I meet many product managers who hate any product idea that the engineers say they need additional time to investigate.

Many of our best product ideas are based on approaches to solving the problem that are only now possible, which means new technology and time to investigate and learn that technology.

To these product managers, this means it is already too risky and time consuming if that happens.

I tell these product managers that I personally love these items for a few reasons. First, many of our best product ideas are based on approaches to solving the problem that are *only now possible*, which means new technology and time to investigate and learn that technology. Second, I find that when engineers are given even a day or two to investigate, they often come back not only with good answers to the feasibility question but also with better ways to solve the problem. Third, these sorts of items are often very motivating to the team, as it gives them an opportunity to learn and to shine.

Discovery for Hardware Products

So many technology-powered products today have a hardware element within them. From phones to watches to robotics to cars to medical instruments to thermostats, smart devices are all around us.

> *With hardware, the consequences of a mistake in terms of time and money are much more severe.*

So how does adding hardware to the equation affect everything we've discussed thus far?

There are some obvious differences, such as different engineering skill sets, the need for industrial design, and of course, manufacturing still takes substantially longer than software, although it continues to improve.

For the most part, however, everything we have discussed thus far still applies, although there are some additional challenges as well. Moreover, when hardware is a part of the equation, the discovery techniques we've discussed are even more important, especially the role of prototyping.

The reason is because, with hardware, the consequences of a mistake in terms of time and money are much more severe. With software, we can usually issue corrections relatively inexpensively. With hardware, no such luck.

(continued)

(continued)

Specifically, there are more technical feasibility risks with hardware, and there are additional business viability risks. For example, with hardware we need a much more sophisticated analysis of parts, manufacturing costs, and forecasting. That said, the necessary prototyping of the hardware device has been helped dramatically with the advent of 3D printing technology.

The bottom line is that hardware products require tackling the value, usability, feasibility, and viability risks aggressively and raising your bar on the level of confidence you have before you commit to manufacturing.

56

Testing Business Viability

There's no question that it's hard enough just trying to come up with a product that your customers love and your engineers can build and deliver. Many products never get to this point.

However, the truth is this is not enough. The solution must also *work for your business*. And I will warn you now that this is often much more difficult than it sounds.

Many product managers confess to me that this is the least favorite part of their job. While I understand that, I also explain to them that this is often what separates the good product managers from the great ones, and that more than anything else, this is what is really meant by being *the CEO of the product*.

Building a business is always hard. You must have a business model that's viable. The costs to produce, market and sell your product must be sufficiently less than the revenue your product generates. You must operate within the laws of the countries you sell in. You must hold up your end of business agreements and partnerships. Your product must fit within the brand promise of your company's other offerings.

You need to help protect your company's revenue, reputation, employees, and customers you've worked so hard to earn.

> *This is what is really meant by being the CEO of the product.*

In this chapter, I name the main stakeholders in a tech-powered product company, discuss their typical concerns and constraints, and explain how the product manager would test business viability with each area.

While this is a very common list, and most or all of these areas probably apply to your products, it is also very common that any company will have one or more special stakeholders that are unique to the business. Just because it's not listed below does not mean it's not absolutely critical for you to deal with.

The last thing you want to have happen is that your team moves forward and takes the time to commercialize the solution and deliver a shippable product, only to find out that you can't ship because you are violating one of these constraints. Make no mistake about it, when that happens, it's on the product manager. It is your job to ensure that you understand each of the relevant constraints, and take positive action to work within them.

Marketing

We've already discussed product marketing, which we view more as a member of the product team than as a stakeholder. But, more generally, marketing cares about enabling sales, they care about the brand and reputation of the company, and they care about market competitiveness and differentiation. Marketing needs the resulting products to be relevant and compelling, and work with the go-to market channels. So, anything that you're considering that puts those at risk will be a major concern.

If what you are proposing to build could impact the sales channel, the major marketing programs, or is potentially outside of the brand promise (the range of things your customers expect from your company), then you'll want to discuss this with marketing and show them prototypes of what you are proposing *before* you consider building anything. Work with them to find ways to address their concerns.

Sales

If your company has a direct sales organization or an advertising sales organization, then this has a very big impact on the product organization. Successful products typically need to be designed around the strengths and limitations of the sales channel.

For example, a direct sales channel is very expensive, and this requires a high-value product and price point. Or, you may have built up a sales channel with a certain set of skills, and if your new product requires a very different set of skills and knowledge, your sales force may completely reject the product.

If what you are proposing would represent a departure from what the sales channel has proven their ability to sell, sit down with the sales leadership and show them what you are proposing *before* you build anything, and see if together you can figure out a way to effectively sell this.

Customer Success

Some tech companies have what's referred to as a *high-touch* model of helping their customers, and some have a *low-touch* model. You need to understand what your company's customer success strategy is, and you need to ensure that your products are aligned with that strategy.

Again, if you are proposing something that would represent a change, you'll want to sit down with leadership and discuss the options.

As a side note, if you have a high-touch service model, these people are exceptionally helpful for product insights and prototype testing.

Finance

Finance often represents several different constraints and considerations, not the least of which is whether you can afford to build, sell, and operate your new product. But, business analytics and reporting are often in finance, and investor relations and other concerns may bring their own set of constraints.

If there are cost issues involved, sitting down with someone in finance and modeling the costs will be critical to demonstrating to leadership that you have worked out a viable approach.

Legal

For many tech-powered companies, especially those that are working hard to disrupt markets, legal can play a very significant role. Privacy concerns, compliance concerns, intellectual property, and competitive issues are all common constraints related to legal. You can save yourself a whole lot of time and grief by sitting down early with someone from your legal team and discussing with them what you are proposing and whether they anticipate any issues or areas you should be aware of.

Business Development

Most businesses have some number of close business relationships with partners of various types, usually with a contract behind each that has a defined set of commitments and constraints. Sometimes these agreements can cripple your company's ability to compete. Sometimes they are a huge win. In either case, you need to understand the impact of these relationships on your products and what you are proposing to do.

Security

We would normally think of security not as a stakeholder, but more as an integral part of the engineering organization and hence a part of the product team. However, the issues involving security are so important for so many technology-powered companies that I think it's useful to call the area out. If you are proposing anything at all remotely related to security, you will probably want to bring your tech lead and sit down with the security leadership early to discuss the ideas and how you will address their concerns.

CEO/COO/GM

Of course, with every company there is some CEO or general manager that is responsible for the business unit. They are very likely aware of all these constraints, and normally they are worried about them. And if the product manager is not also aware of the issues, or does not have a plan for dealing with them, the exec is not going to trust the product manager or product team.

It doesn't take long for a CEO to figure out whether a product manager has done her homework and understands the different aspects of the business.

Testing business viability means making sure that the product solution that your team is proposing will work within the constraints of each of these areas. For those stakeholders that are impacted, it's important that they have a chance to review the proposal and ensure their concerns have been addressed.

User Test versus Product Demo versus Walkthrough

Throughout this book, I have talked about "showing the prototype." In truth, there are three very different techniques for showing the prototype, and you have to be careful to use the right technique for the right situation.

A *user test* is when we *test* our product ideas on real users and customers. It is a qualitative usability and value-testing technique, and we let the user drive. The purpose is to *test* the usability and value of the prototype or product.

A *product demo* is when you *sell* your product to prospective users and customers, or evangelize your product across your company. This is a sales or persuasive tool. Product marketing usually creates a carefully scripted product demo, but the product manager will occasionally be asked to give the product demo—especially with high-value customers or execs. In this case, the product manager does the driving. The purpose is to *show off* the value of the prototype or product.

(continued)

(continued)

A *walkthrough* is when you show your prototype to a stakeholder and you want to make sure they see and note absolutely everything that might be a concern. The purpose is to give the stakeholder every opportunity to spot a

> *There are three very different techniques for showing the prototype, and you have to be careful to use the right technique for the right situation.*

problem. The product manager usually drives, but if the stakeholder would like to play with the prototype we are happy to let them. You are not trying to sell them anything, you're not trying to test on them, and you're *definitely* not trying to hide anything from them.

I have seen many inexperienced product managers do a walkthrough with a prospective customer when they should have prepared a product demo. Or another really common rookie mistake is to do a product demo during a user test, and then ask the user what they think.

Be sure to be clear about whether you're doing a user test, a product demo, or a walkthrough. And, be sure you're skilled in how to do all three.

57

Profile: Kate Arnold of Netflix

N etflix is one of my all-time favorite products and companies. But back in 1999, a then very young Netflix—based in Los Gatos, with fewer than 20 employees—was on the edge of going bust. They had a couple of experienced co-founders, including the now legendary Reed Hastings, but the problem was that they were stuck at about 300,000 customers.

They were essentially providing the same general pay-per-rental experience that Blockbuster provided, just an online version. There were, as always, some early adopters, and some people lived in places that didn't have a video store, but in truth there wasn't much of a reason to rent DVDs via the U.S. Postal Service when you could just stop by the local Blockbuster store on the way home from work. People would rent once from Netflix and then quickly forget about the service. They didn't seem very willing to change. The team knew that the service wasn't better enough to get people to change.

Even worse, DVD sales were starting to lag, and a Hollywood backlash further muddied the situation. Then there were challenges with fulfillment logistics, difficulty maintaining DVD quality, and trying to figure out how to do all this in a way that covered costs and generated some cash.

> *Those were the technology-powered innovations that enabled the new, much more desirable business model.*

Kate Arnold was the product manager for this small team, and the team knew they needed to do something different.

One of many tests they tried was to move to a subscription service. The idea was to get people to sign up for a month, and offer them unlimited movies. Would that be perceived as better enough to get them to change their media consumption behavior?

The *good news* was that, yes, this approach really did appeal to people. A flat monthly fee and all the videos they could consume sounded pretty great.

The *bad news* is that the team created some real problems for themselves. No surprise that Netflix customers wanted to rent mostly newly released feature films; yet, these were much more expensive for Netflix to stock, and they would need to stock so many copies of these that they'd very likely run out of money fast.

So, the product challenge became how they were going to make sure Netflix customers could watch a set of movies they would love, yet wouldn't bankrupt the company.

They knew they needed to somehow get customers to want and ask for a blend of expensive and less expensive titles. Necessity being the mother of invention, this is where Netflix's queue, ratings system, and recommendation engine all came from. Those were the technology-powered innovations that *enabled* the new, much more desirable business model.

So, the team got to work. In three months' time, the team redesigned the site—introducing the queue, the rating system, and the recommendations engine all in support of Netflix as a subscription service.

They also rewrote the billing system to handle the monthly subscription model (a funny little side story is that they launched without this, as they had the 30-day free trial month, which bought them the extra time they needed).

With so many moving pieces and interconnected efforts, the daily standups included just about every person in the company.

Between working with the co-founders on the strategy, validating concepts with the users, assessing the analytics, driving features and functionality with the team—and working with finance on the new business model, marketing on acquisition, and the warehouse on fulfillment—you can imagine the workload Kate faced on a daily basis. Yet, the team got the new service up and running and used this to power and grow their business for another seven years, until they disrupted themselves again by moving aggressively to the streaming model.

Kate would be the first to credit a pretty amazing team, including some exceptional engineers, and the vision and courage of the founders. But I would argue that without Kate driving for the technology-based solutions that could power this business, there's a good chance Netflix as we know it never would have happened.

One more interesting little aside about early Netflix—when they were struggling for cash early on, they offered to sell themselves to Blockbuster for $50 million, and Blockbuster turned them down. Today, Blockbuster is in the dead pool, and Netflix is worth more than $40 *billion*.

Kate is now a product leader in New York City.

Transformation Techniques

Overview

So far, we've been discussing techniques for discovering successful products. But it's important to acknowledge that getting product teams and companies to apply the new techniques and work differently is often easier said than done.

Partly this is because people are people. But mainly it's hard because the changes are so often cultural.

As a very explicit example, moving from mercenary-style, product roadmap-driven, output-focused teams, to truly empowered, accountable product teams that are measured by business results, represents a major cultural shift and a substantial handoff of power and control from management to the individuals on the teams.

Believe me, this is not the type of change that happens easily.

Fortunately, there are techniques that can help the organization through this.

58

Discovery Sprint Technique

I find that many teams, especially those new to modern product techniques, are looking for a structured introduction to modern product discovery. In this chapter, I describe the concept of a *discovery sprint*.

A *discovery sprint* is a one-week time box of product discovery work, designed to tackle a substantial problem or risk your product team is facing.

A discovery sprint is definitely useful for more than just transformation. It could just as easily be considered a discovery planning technique or a discovery prototyping technique. But I find it's most helpful in bringing all these things together, so I choose to include it here.

Some people use the term *design sprint* rather than *discovery sprint*, but as the purpose of the work—when done well—goes significantly beyond design, I prefer the more general term.

Further, if your company has been struggling with the concept of MVP, this is a very good way to start getting the value from this key technique.

I first met the Google Ventures (GV) team many years ago when they were just getting started. They are part of Google's investment arm, but even more valuable to the startup than their money, GV created a small team to go in and help the companies they invest in get their product efforts off to a good start. Their model is to typically spend a week with the startup—rolling up their sleeves and showing them how to do product discovery by doing it with them side by side.

> *A discovery sprint is a one-week time box of product discovery work, designed to tackle a substantial problem or risk your product team is facing.*

I also know several other proven product people, known as *discovery coaches*, who do essentially the same thing for the teams they are helping.

In any case, during this week of intense discovery work, you and your team will likely explore dozens of different product ideas and approaches, with the goal of solving some significant business problem. You'll always end your week by validating your potential solution with real users and customers. And, in my experience, the result is consistently big learning and insights—the kind of learning that can change the course of your product or your company.

Within this general framework, discovery coaches advocate a variety of different methods to help the team though the process and get big learning in just five days.

After working with more than 100 product teams, and refining their methods as they learned what worked well and what didn't, the GV team decided to share their learnings in a book. The book is titled, *Sprint: How to Solve Big Problems and Test New Ideas in Just Five Days*, by Jake Knapp, John Zeratsky, and Braden Kowitz.

The authors lay out a five-day week that starts with framing the problem by mapping the problem space, picking the problem to be solved and the target customer, and then progresses into pursuing several different approaches to the solution. The team next narrows down and fleshes out the different potential solutions, then creates a high-fidelity user prototype—finally, putting that prototype in front of actual target users and observing their reactions.

And, yes, you can absolutely do this all in a week.

Sprint spells out the authors' favorite techniques to accomplish each of these steps, and if you've read this far, you'll recognize all of them. But what I like so much about the GV book is that, when teams are getting started, they often crave the structure of a proven, step-by-step recipe. The book spells out exactly this over nearly 300 pages, with dozens of examples from great products and teams you'll recognize.

There are several situations where I recommend a discovery sprint, starting with when the team has something big and critically important and/or difficult to tackle. Another situation where a discovery sprint helps is when the team is just learning how to do product discovery. And yet another is when things are just moving too slow and the team needs to recalibrate on just how fast they can and should be moving.

Sprint is another must read book for product managers, and I highly recommend it.

Discovery Coaches

As teams moved to Agile methods (they usually start with Scrum), many companies decided to contract with or hire an Agile coach. These coaches help the broader team—especially engineers, QA, product managers, and product designers—learn the methods and mindset involved in moving to Agile.

> *Discovery coaches are typically former product managers or product designers and they have usually worked for, or with, leading product companies.*

This sounds straightforward enough, but many problems arise because the vast majority of these Agile coaches don't have experience with tech-product companies, so their experience is limited to delivery. Therefore, they would more accurately be considered Agile delivery coaches. They understand the engineering and release side of things, but not the discovery side of things.

(continued)

(continued)

So many product companies have experienced this issue that it created the need for coaches that do have deep experience with product companies and the key product roles, especially product management and product design. These individuals are often called *discovery coaches*.

Discovery coaches are typically former product managers or product designers (or former leaders of these areas) and they have usually worked for, or with, leading product companies. So, they are able to work side by side with actual product managers and designers—not just reciting Agile platitudes, but showing the team how to work effectively.

Every discovery coach has his or her preferred way of engaging with a team, but they are usually engaged with one or a small number of product teams for a week or so. During this time, they help you through one or more discovery cycles of ideation; creating prototypes; and validating the prototypes with customers to gauge their reactions, with engineers to evaluate feasibility, and with business stakeholders to assess whether this solution would work for your business.

It's hard for me to imagine an effective discovery coach who doesn't have first-hand experience as a product manager or product designer at a modern product company. That's likely one of the main reasons there's a shortage of discovery coaches today. It's also important that the discovery coach understand how to include engineering in the mix—being sensitive to their time, but understanding the essential role they play in innovation.

Discovery coaches are not unlike Lean Startup coaches. The main difference is that Lean Startup coaches often focus on helping a team discover not only their product, but also their business model, and their sales and marketing strategy. Once the new business has some traction, the discovery is usually more about continuously improving an existing product in substantial ways rather than creating an all-new business. Because of this difference, many Lean Startup coaches don't have the necessary product experience. My view is that product discovery is the most important competency of a new startup, so I believe an effective Lean Startup coach must also be very strong at product.

59

Pilot Team Technique

Earlier in this book, we discussed the technology adoption curve and how this theory describes how different people will accept change. It turns out this theory also applies to our own organization and especially to how we make changes to how that organization works.

Some people in your organization love change, some want to see someone else use it successfully first, some need more time to digest changes, and a few hate change and will only change if they're forced to do it.

If you get too excited and roll out a significant change to everyone in the organization at once, then the laggards (those that hate change) may resist or even sabotage your efforts.

Rather than fight this reality, we can embrace it. One of the simplest techniques for facilitating moving to new ways of working is the use of pilot teams. *Pilot teams* allow the roll out of change to a limited part of the organization before implementing it more broadly. The idea is that you look for a product team to volunteer to try out some new techniques. You let them run for a while (usually a quarter or two) with this new way of working and see how this goes.

Your specific success measures will depend on your goals, but ultimately, you're looking to compare the team's effectiveness in delivering business outcomes; that is, how well do the pilot teams accomplish their objectives versus the others or compared to how they did in the past?

Some people in your organization love change, some want to see someone else use it successfully first, some need more time to digest changes, and a few hate change and will only change if they're forced to do it.

Given the nature of the experiment, your comparisons will be qualitative, but that doesn't make them any less compelling.

If things go well, you'll likely end up with several other teams eager to adopt. If things don't go well, you might decide this technique is not a fit for you, or you might decide to make adjustments.

To maximize the chance of the pilot teams having a good outcome, we carefully consider the people involved, their location, and their degree of autonomy. Ideally, we have people who are open to new ways of working, the key people on the team are co-located, and the team is largely in control of how they work and not so dependent on other teams that still work in the old way.

60

Weaning an Organization Off Roadmaps

Many product teams want to move off product roadmaps, but their organizations are old school, addicted to the outdated quarterly product roadmap. As a result, they don't see how to transition their organizations forward.

Here's what I advocate in this case: Plan to continue with your existing roadmap process for six to 12 months. However, starting immediately, every time you reference a product roadmap item, or discuss it in a presentation or meeting, be sure to include a reminder of the actual *business outcome* that feature is intended to help.

If the feature you're working on is to add PayPal as a payment method, and the reason is to increase conversion, then be sure to always show the current conversion rate and the result you're hoping

> *The goal is that over time, the organization moves its focus from specific features launching on specific dates to business results.*

to achieve. Most important, after the feature goes live, be sure to highlight the impact on that conversion rate.

If the impact was good, celebrate it. If the impact was not what was hoped, then emphasize to everyone that, while you did ship the feature, the result was not successful. Point out specifically what was learned, but explain that you have other ideas for ways to get the desired result.

The goal is that over time (it can take as long as a year), the organization moves its focus from specific features launching on specific dates to business results.

For this to work, it's important to acknowledge the two big reasons why stakeholders especially are so attracted to roadmaps:

1. They want some visibility into what you are working on and assurance that you are working on the most important items.
2. They want to be able to plan the business and need to know when critical things will happen.

The modern alternative to roadmaps discussed here addresses both of these concerns. Teams work on the prioritized business objectives determined by the leaders; we share our key results transparently; and we commit to high-integrity commitments when critical delivery dates are needed.

Process @ Scale

Overview

It is understandable that, as companies grow, they become more risk averse. When you're small there really isn't much to lose, but as you get to scale, there is quite a lot on the line, and many people from across the company are there to try to protect those assets.

One way companies try to protect what they've achieved is to institute process by formalizing and standardizing how things are done in the name of reducing error or risk. This applies from how we get reimbursed for travel expenses, to how we request a change to a report, to how we discover and deliver product.

> *It is all too easy to institute processes that govern how you produce products that can bring innovation to a grinding halt.*

In many areas, such as expense reporting, it's an irritant but not likely to make the difference between success and failure of the company.

On the other hand, it is all too easy to institute processes that govern how you produce products that can bring innovation to a grinding halt. Nobody does this intentionally, but it happens so frequently, in so many companies, that I find it quite remarkable.

As just one example in the process area, Agile methods are generally very conducive to consistent innovation. Yet there are several process consultancies that specialize in "Agile at Scale," which introduce methods and structures intended to scale to large numbers of engineers, yet which absolutely destroy any hope of innovation.

It does not have to be this way. Many of the best product companies in the world are very large companies that have successfully scaled their product and technology organizations. The techniques and methods described here are all about maintaining your ability to consistently innovate as you continue to grow and scale.

61

Managing Stakeholders

For many product managers, managing stakeholders is probably the least favorite part of their job. I don't want to suggest that this will always be easy, but it can usually be substantially improved.

First, let's consider just who is a stakeholder, then what the product manager's responsibilities are with these stakeholders. After that, we'll talk about techniques for success.

Stakeholder Defined

In many product companies, just about anyone and everyone feels like they have a say in the products. They certainly care about the product, and they often have many ideas—either derived from their own use, or from what they hear from customers. But, regardless of what *they* think, we would not consider most of them to be stakeholders. They are just part of the community at large—another source of input on the product, along with many others.

One practical test of whether a person is considered a stakeholder is whether or not they have veto power, or can otherwise prevent your work from launching.

This group of people typically includes:

- The executive team (CEO and leaders of marketing, sales, and technology)
- Business partners (to make sure the product and the business are aligned)
- Finance (to make sure the product fits within the financial parameters and model of the company)
- Legal (to make sure that what you propose is defensible)
- Compliance (to make sure what you propose complies with any relevant standards or policies)
- Business development (to make sure what you propose does not violate any existing contracts or relationships)

There can be others, but you get the idea.

In a startup, there are few stakeholders because the company is very small, and frankly, there's not a lot to lose. But in large companies, quite a few people are there to protect the substantial assets of the company.

Product Manager Responsibilities

In terms of the stakeholders, the product manager has the responsibility to understand the considerations and constraints of the various stakeholders, and to bring this knowledge into the product team. It doesn't do anyone any good to build things that may work for the customer, but then at some review meeting find out that you're not allowed to deploy what was created. This happens much more than you might

realize, and every time it does happen, the company loses a little more
confidence in the product team.

The product manager has the responsibility to understand the considerations and constraints of the various stakeholders, and to bring this knowledge into the product team.

However, beyond understanding the constraints and concerns
of each stakeholder, if you want
the latitude to come up with the
most-effective solutions, then it's
critically important that the product manager convince each of these
stakeholders that she not only understands the issues, but that she is
committed to coming up with solutions that not only work for the
customer, but also work for the stakeholder as well. And this must be
sincere. I emphasize this because, if the stakeholder does not have this
trust that you are going to solve for their concerns as well, then they
will either escalate, or they will try to control.

Strategies for Success

Success in terms of stakeholder management means that your
stakeholders respect you and your contribution. They trust that you
understand their concerns and will ensure solutions work well for
them too. They trust that you will keep them informed of important
decisions or changes. And, most of all, they give you the room to come
up with the best solutions possible, even when those solutions end up
being quite different from what they might have originally envisioned.

It's not that difficult to have this kind of relationship with stakeholders, but it does require first and foremost that you are a competent
product manager. This especially means having a deep understanding
of your customers, the analytics, the technology, your industry, and in
particular, your business.

Without this, they won't trust you (and in fairness they shouldn't).
The main way we demonstrate this knowledge to the organization is
by sharing very openly what we learn.

With this as a foundation, the key technique is to spend one-on-one time with the key stakeholders. Sit down with them and listen. Explain that the better you understand their constraints, the better your solutions will be. Ask lots of questions. Be open and transparent.

One of the most common mistakes product managers make with stakeholders is that they show them their solution after they have already built it. And, sometimes, there are issues because the product manager did not have a clear enough understanding of the constraints. Not only will the stakeholder be frustrated, but your engineering team will be frustrated as well with all the rework. So, commit to previewing your solutions during discovery with the key stakeholders *before* you put this work on the product backlog.

This is one of the keys of product discovery. In discovery, you are not only making sure that your solutions are valuable and usable (with customers), and feasible (with engineers), but you are also making sure your stakeholders will support the proposed solution.

The other big mistake I often see being made is when situations boil down to the product manager's opinion versus the stakeholder's opinion. In this case, the stakeholder usually wins because he or she is usually more senior. However, as we've already discussed many times before, the key is to change the game by quickly running a test and collecting some evidence. Move the discussion from opinions to data. Share what you're learning very openly. It may be that neither of your opinions were right. Again, the discovery work is designed specifically as a place for these tests.

Mostly this is about creating a collaborative, mutually respectful personal relationship. For most companies, it takes about two to three hours a week—meeting for half an hour or so with each key stakeholder—to keep them apprised, and to get their feedback on new ideas. My favorite way to do this is a weekly lunch or coffee with your most-involved stakeholders.

Many product managers tell me that the way they deal with testing business viability with all their different stakeholders is by scheduling a large, group meeting and inviting all the stakeholders. The product manager then presents to them what they want to build, usually with a PowerPoint presentation.

There are two very serious (potentially career limiting) problems with this.

First, presentations are notoriously terrible for testing business viability. The reason is that they are far too ambiguous. A lawyer needs to see the actual proposed screens, pages, and wording. A marketing leader wants to see the actual product design. A security leader needs to see exactly what the product is trying to do. Presentations are terrible for this.

In contrast, high-fidelity user prototypes are *ideal* for this. I plead with product managers in larger companies to not trust a sign-off on anything other than a high-fidelity prototype. I have seen far too many times where the execs agree to something based on a presentation, but when they see the actual product, they are completely shocked, frustrated, and often visibly angry.

The second problem is that a group setting is not the forum for designing strong products. It results in design by committee, which yields mediocre results at best. Instead, meet privately with each stakeholder, show them the high-fidelity prototype, and give them the chance to raise any concerns.

This may sound like more work to you, but please believe me that, in the long run, it will turn out to be far less work, time, and grief.

One final note: in many companies, some of the stakeholders may not even understand what product does, and some may even feel threatened by the role. Be sensitive to this. You may need to spend some time explaining the role and how technology-enabled product companies operate and why.

Devolving from Good to Bad

Lots of people have written about the challenges of managing growth, and especially about the importance of working hard to maintain staff quality as you scale the organization.

There is little question that most organizations become worse in their ability to rapidly deliver consistent innovation as they grow, yet most people attribute this to staff quality, process, and communication issues of scale. Some believe that this is unavoidable.

(continued)

(continued)

There's an anti-pattern I see in many companies that are doing very well, growing aggressively, yet they will sometimes—over time and unintentionally—replace their good behaviors with bad ones.

I have never seen this anti-pattern written about before, and I suspect it's going to make more than a few people uncomfortable. But it's a serious issue that I think needs to be out in the open, as it's not hard to prevent if you're aware.

The scenario is that you are probably a later-stage startup or growth-stage company. You've probably achieved product/market fit, at least for an initial product, and to have accomplished that, you've probably done some important things right. But then you get some substantial funding, or a board member strongly suggests that you need to bring on some "adult supervision" or some experienced people from brand-name companies.

Here's the thing. The new people you hire are often from those large, brand-name companies that have stopped growing, have long since lost their ability to innovate, and have been living off their brand for many years. Because of this, they're not on the trajectory they once were, and people leave.

Would you rather hire all your staff and leaders from Google, Facebook, Amazon, and Netflix? Sure you would, but these people are in very short supply and there is lots of strong talent at other companies.

But, let's say you are at a young, growth-stage company, and you decide to hire a senior leader—maybe the head of product, or the head of engineering, or the head of marketing—from a brand name like Oracle. Your board will probably like that.

> *There is little question that most organizations become worse in their ability to rapidly deliver consistent innovation as they grow, yet most people attribute this to staff quality, process, and communication issues of scale.*

(continued)

(continued)

The issue is that, unless you make this clear at the outset, that new leader may assume you're hiring them for their knowledge of process and how to define and deliver products. And, so they bring with them their views on how things should work. Even worse, they often then proceed to hire people that want to work in those ways.

Note that I'm picking on Oracle here as an example, but they are certainly not the only one. There are a great many very strong people to hire from Oracle as they love to acquire companies, often very good companies, but those strong product, design, and technology people they also acquired rarely like Oracle's culture or ways of creating product.

I have seen this anti-pattern play out at every level of a company—from individual engineers all the way to CEO. It doesn't happen overnight; it happens over years. But I've seen it enough to be convinced it's an anti-pattern. Many people intuitively sense this problem but they usually just attribute it to a "big company person," but this is less about being from a big company and more about being from a company that's not strong at product.

I know of two ways to prevent this problem from infecting your company:

The first is to have a very strong and very intentional product culture, and to have that culture very well established so that new hires know they're joining a different type of company that takes pride in how they work and in using best practices. When you join Netflix, or Airbnb, or Facebook, it's something you figure out in your first days, and that's their intention.

The second way of preventing this is to make this explicit in the interview and onboarding process. As part of my advisory work, I'm often on the interview team for senior positions, and when the person is coming from one of these types of companies, I'm up front with the prospective hire. We'll talk about the reasons why their former company has not produced successful new products in many years, and I'll emphasize to them that the new company is interested in them

(continued)

(continued)

because of their mind and their talents, and of course they wouldn't want to bring with them the bad practices of their former company.

In my experience, people are really good about this when you talk openly and honestly about it. In fact, people often tell me it's a major reason why they want to leave their former company. It's more about getting this to be something you and they are very aware of.

CHAPTER

62

Communicating Product Learnings

Sharing what we learn in a startup happens naturally because the product team and the company are pretty much the same thing. However, as companies scale, this becomes substantially more difficult; yet, it also becomes increasingly important to do.

A technique I love for helping with this is for the head of product, at a company all-hands or similar meeting every week or two, to take 15 to 30 minutes to highlight what has been learned in product discovery across the various product teams.

Note that this is meant to cover the bigger learnings and not the minor things—what worked, what didn't work, and what the teams are planning to try the following week.

This update needs to move fast and kept at the big learnings level, which is why I prefer the VP product to do this. This is *not* where every product manager parades in front of everyone for a detailed update, taking one to two hours of time and at more detail than most people want to see. It's not meant to be a repeat of sprint reviews either.

Instead, the update is meant to address several purposes, some tactical and some cultural:

- The big learnings are important to share broadly, especially when things don't go as hoped. As a side benefit, sometimes someone in the audience has an insight about what might explain the results.

- This is a useful and easy way for the various product teams to keep apprised of what other teams are learning, as well as ensuring that useful learnings make it to the leaders.

- This technique encourages the product teams to keep their focus on big learnings and not on minor experimentation that doesn't have a real customer or business impact one way or the other.

- Culturally, it's critical that the organization understand that discovery and innovation is about continuously running these rapid experiments and learning from the results.

- It is also important culturally that the product organization be transparent and generous in what they learn and how they work. It helps the broader organization to understand that the product organization is not there "to serve the business" but, rather, to solve problems for our customers in ways that work for our business.

63

Profile: Camille Hearst of Apple

I'd love to introduce you to another very strong product manager, Camille Hearst.

Camille was a product manager on the iTunes team at Apple, and as you might imagine with such a disruptive and groundbreaking product, she experienced and learned a great deal during her formative product years at Apple. This was especially the case because she was there during the years moving from iTunes's original DRM-based music to DRM-free, which was critical in helping iTunes become truly mass market.

Moving beyond early adopters into mass market involved many different efforts, some product, some marketing, and some a blend of the two. A good example of this blend was the relationship the iTunes team engaged with the *American Idol* television program.

This turned out to be one of the most dramatic and visible—yet challenging—product efforts for the iTunes team.

During 2008, *American Idol* was a cultural icon—watched by more than 25 million people twice a week, with a level of repeat engagement that was largely unrivaled.

Apple saw in this an opportunity to expose an ideal target market

This is a great example of how great product managers work to find creative solutions to very difficult problems.

to the power of iTunes and digital music. Not just by selling the music from the contestants featured on the show but by making iTunes an integral part of consumers' lives.

However, while the potential was substantial, the challenges were significant as well.

The VP of iTunes, Eddy Cue, and others made the business deal, but Camille worked as product manager on many of the integrations to help figure this out.

As just one example, the *American Idol* program is all about voting, and Apple quickly realized that sales of contestants' music would very likely be strongly indicative of voting results. So, while normally iTunes was designed to show trending music and highlight popular titles, in this case, it was important to use extreme care *not* to influence the voting.

This was obviously critically important to the *Idol* producers—it would reduce or even eliminate the suspense to learn which contestants would continue to the next week.

The integration also allowed the team to target a very specific persona and work to drive up engagement with this group. One of the keys was to make it easy to get to iTunes for those that didn't yet have the app installed.

By tackling these and countless other challenges head-on, Camille and her team came up with technology solutions that complemented the *American Idol* experience, yet also injected iTunes as a key component of fans' lives. This contributed to what was in 2014, before the move to streaming, a roughly *$20 billion* business.

To me, this is a great example of how great product managers work to find creative solutions to very difficult problems.

Camille went on to join the YouTube team and then lead product at London-based Hailo. Now I'm very happy to say that she's CEO of a NYC-based startup.

V

The Right Culture

We've worked through quite a lot of information, and I believe it would useful at this point to step back and consider the range and scope of how the product manager role is defined, how these people work collaboratively with their product team, and the techniques they use to quickly come up with products worth building and delivering to customers.

It's easy to get hung up on the minutiae of all this, but what's really important here is creating the right *product culture* for success.

In these final chapters, I'll push your focus to what's most important to your success. In particular, how does a great product team behave, and how do strong product companies provide these teams with an environment where they can flourish?

CHAPTER

64

Good Product Team/Bad Product Team

I've had the extremely good fortune to be able to work with many of the best technology product teams in the world—the people creating the products you use and love every day, teams that are literally changing the world.

I've also been brought in to try to help with companies that are not doing so well. Startups racing to get some traction before the money runs out. Larger companies struggling to replicate their early innovation. Teams failing to continuously add value to their business. Leaders frustrated with how long it takes to go from idea to reality. Engineers exasperated with their product managers.

What I've learned is that there is a profound difference between how the very best product companies create technology products and all the rest. And I don't mean minor differences. Everything from how the leaders behave to the level of empowerment of teams to how the organization thinks about funding, staffing, and

producing products, down to how
product, design, and engineering
collaborate to discover effective
solutions for their customers.

> *Good teams have a
> compelling product vision
> that they pursue with a
> missionary-like passion.
> Bad teams are mercenaries.*

With a grateful nod to Ben
Horowitz's classic post "Good
Product Manager/Bad Product
Manager," for those that have not yet had the opportunity to participate in or observe a strong product team up close, in this chapter I
provide you with a glimpse into some of the important differences
between strong product teams and weak teams:

- Good teams have a compelling product vision that they pursue
  with a missionary-like passion. Bad teams are mercenaries.

- Good teams get their inspiration and product ideas from their
  vision and objectives, from observing customers' struggle, from
  analyzing the data customers generate from using their product,
  and from constantly seeking to apply new technology to solve
  real problems. Bad teams gather requirements from sales and customers.

- Good teams understand who each of their key stakeholders are,
  they understand the constraints that these stakeholders operate in,
  and they are committed to inventing solutions that work not just
  for users and customers, but also work within the constraints of
  the business. Bad teams gather requirements from stakeholders.

- Good teams are skilled in the many techniques to rapidly try out
  product ideas to determine which ones are truly worth building.
  Bad teams hold meetings to generate prioritized roadmaps.

- Good teams love to have brainstorming discussions with smart
  thought leaders from across the company. Bad teams get offended
  when someone outside their team dares to suggest they do
  something.

- Good teams have product, design, and engineering sit side by side,
  and they embrace the give and take between the functionality, the
  user experience, and the enabling technology. Bad teams sit in
  their respective silos, and ask that others make requests for their
  services in the form of documents and scheduling meetings.

- Good teams are constantly trying out new ideas to innovate, but doing so in ways that protect the revenue and protect the brand. Bad teams are still waiting for permission to run a test.

- Good teams insist they have the skill sets on their team, such as strong product design, necessary to create winning products. Bad teams don't even know what product designers are.

- Good teams ensure that their engineers have time to try out the prototypes in discovery every day so that they can contribute their thoughts on how to make the product better. Bad teams show the prototypes to the engineers during sprint planning so they can estimate.

- Good teams engage directly with end users and customers every week, to better understand their customers, and to see the customer's response to their latest ideas. Bad teams think they are the customer.

- Good teams know that many of their favorite ideas won't end up working for customers, and even the ones that could will need several iterations to get to the point where they provide the desired outcome. Bad teams just build what's on the roadmap, and are satisfied with meeting dates and ensuring quality.

- Good teams understand the need for speed and how rapid iteration is the key to innovation, and they understand this speed comes from the right techniques and not forced labor. Bad teams complain they are slow because their colleagues are not working hard enough.

- Good teams make high-integrity commitments after they've evaluated the request and ensured they have a viable solution that will work for the customer and the business. Bad teams complain about being a sales-driven company.

- Good teams instrument their work so they can immediately understand how their product is being used and make adjustments based on the data. Bad teams consider analytics and reporting a nice to have.

- Good teams integrate and release continuously, knowing that a constant stream of smaller releases provides a much more stable solution for their customers. Bad teams test manually at the end of a painful integration phase and then release everything at once.

- Good teams obsess over their reference customers. Bad teams obsess over their competitors.

- Good teams celebrate when they achieve a significant impact to the business results. Bad teams celebrate when they finally release something.

If a significant number of these items strike too close to home, I hope you'll consider raising the bar for your team. See if you can't use the techniques in this book to experience the difference.

65

Top Reasons for Loss of Innovation

I define *consistent innovation* as the ability of a team to repeatedly add value to the business. Many organizations lose their ability to innovate at scale, and this is incredibly frustrating to both leaders and the members of the product teams. It's one of the main reasons people often leave large companies for startups.

But losing the ability to innovate is absolutely and demonstrably not inevitable. Some of the most consistently innovative companies in our industry are very large—consider Amazon, Google, Facebook, and Netflix as examples.

Organizations that lose the ability to innovate at scale are inevitably missing one or more of the following attributes:

1. **Customer-centric culture.** As Jeff Bezos, the CEO of Amazon says, "Customers are always beautifully, wonderfully dissatisfied, even when they report being happy and business is great. Even when they don't yet know it, customers want something better,

and your desire to delight customers will drive you to invent on their behalf." Companies that don't have this focus on customers—and direct and frequent contact with them—lose this passion and critical source of inspiration.

> *"Customers are always beautifully, wonderfully dissatisfied, even when they report being happy and business is great. Even when they don't yet know it, customers want something better, and your desire to delight customers will drive you to invent on their behalf."*

2. **Compelling product vision.** By the time many companies reach scale, their original product vision is now largely realized, and the team is struggling to understand what's next. This is often compounded because the original founders may have moved on, and they were likely the keepers of the vision. In this case, someone else—usually either the CEO or the VP product—needs to step up and fill this void.

3. **Focused product strategy.** One of the surest paths to product failure is to try to please everyone at once. Yet large companies often forget this reality. The product strategy needs to spell out a logical and intentional sequence of target markets for the product teams to focus on.

4. **Strong product managers.** The lack of a strong and capable product manager is typically a major reason for lack of product innovation. When a company is small, the CEO or one of the co-founders usually plays this role, but at scale, each product team depends on a strong and capable product manager.

5. **Stable product teams.** One of the prerequisites for consistent innovation is a team that has had a chance to learn the space, technologies, and customer pain. This doesn't happen if the members of the team are constantly shifting.

6. **Engineers in discovery.** So often the key to innovation is the engineers on the team, but this means (a) including them from the very beginning, and not just at the end and (b) exposing them directly to the customer pain.

7. **Corporate courage.** It's no secret that many companies become extremely risk averse as they grow larger. There is, of course, much more to lose. But the best technology-product companies know that the riskiest strategy of all is to stop taking risks. We do have to be smart about how we work, but the willingness to risk disruption to our current business is essential to consistent innovation.

8. **Empowered product teams.** Even though your organization might have begun by using best practices, many organizations regress as they scale, and if you've reverted to just handing your teams roadmaps of features, then you no longer can expect the benefits of empowered product teams. Remember that empowerment means the teams are able to tackle and solve the business problems they've been assigned in the best way they see fit.

9. **Product mindset.** In an IT-mindset organization, the product teams exist to serve the needs of the business. In contrast, in a product-mind set organization, the product teams exist to serve the company's customers in ways that meet the needs of the business. The resulting differences between these mind sets are many and profound.

10. **Time to innovate.** At scale, it's very possible that your product teams are entirely consumed just doing what we call *keep the lights on* activities. Fixing bugs, implementing capabilities for different parts of the business, addressing technical debt, and more. If this is your situation, you shouldn't be surprised at the lack of innovation. Some of this is normal and healthy, but be sure that your teams have the room to also pursue harder and more impactful problems.

I hope you notice that the above list essentially describes a culture of consistent innovation. It's much more about culture than it is about process—or anything else.

CHAPTER

66

Top Reasons for Loss of Velocity

As organizations grow, it's not unusual for things to slow down. They don't need to, and in the best organizations, they can accelerate. But if you are seeing a slowdown, these are the first things to look for.

1. **Technical debt.** Often, the architecture does not facilitate or enable the rapid evolution of the product. This is not something that can be fixed overnight, but it needs to be attacked in an ongoing and concerted effort.

2. **Lack of strong product managers.** The lack of a strong and capable product manager is typically a major reason for slow product. The impact of a weak product manager shows up in many ways, but it shows up very visibly as a team of mercenaries rather than missionaries. The product manager has not inspired or evangelized to the team, or the team has lost confidence in their product manager.

319

3. **Lack of delivery management.** The most important function of the delivery manager is to remove impediments, and the list of impediments grows non-linearly

> *The lack of a strong and capable product manager is typically a major reason for slow product.*

as the technology organization grows. Most impediments won't go away quickly without someone actively chasing them down.

4. **Infrequent release cycles.** Most teams with slow velocity have release vehicles that are too infrequent. Your team should release no less frequently than every two weeks (very good teams release multiple times per day). Correcting this typically means getting serious about test automation and release automation so the team can move quickly and release with confidence.

5. **Lack of product vision and strategy.** It's essential that the team have a clear vision of the big picture and how their immediate work contributes to the whole.

6. **Lack of co-located, durable product teams.** If teams are split across locations—or worse, if engineers are outsourced—besides the dramatic decrease in innovation, the velocity of the organization will suffer significantly. Even simple communication becomes difficult. It gets so bad that many outsourcing firms will add another layer of people to coordinate and communicate, which usually makes things worse.

7. **Not including engineers early enough during product discovery.** The engineers need to participate in product discovery from the start of ideation. They will often contribute alternative approaches that can be significantly faster to implement if you include them early enough in the process for the product manager and designer to adjust. If not, their critical input will come too late in the process.

8. **Not utilizing product design in discovery and instead having them try to do their work at the same time the engineers are trying to build.** Not doing this will both slow things down and lead to poor designs.

9. **Changing priorities.** Realize that rapidly shifting priorities cause significant churn and substantially reduces the total throughput and morale.

10. **A consensus culture.** Many organizations strive for consensus. While this typically comes from good intentions, what this means in practice is decisions are very hard to make and everything slows to a crawl.

There are, of course, any number of other causes of slow product, but in my experience, these are among the most common culprits.

67

Establishing a Strong Product Culture

While we've talked about product teams and techniques for discovering successful products, I hope you've noticed that what we're really talking about in this book is product *culture*. I've described to you how great product companies think, organize, and operate.

I think of product culture along two dimensions. The first dimension is whether the company can consistently innovate to come up with valuable solutions for their customers. This is what product discovery is all about.

The second dimension is execution. It doesn't matter how great the ideas are if you can't get a productized, shippable version delivered to your customers. This is what product delivery is all about.

My goal in this final chapter is to describe the characteristics of a strong *innovation* culture versus those of a strong *execution* culture.

What does it really mean to have a strong innovation culture?

> *What we're really talking about in this book is product* culture. *I've described to you how great product companies think, organize, and operate.*

- Culture of experimentation—teams know they can run tests; some will succeed and many will fail, and this is acceptable and understood.

- Culture of open minds—teams know that good ideas can come from anywhere and aren't always obvious at the outset.

- Culture of empowerment—individuals and teams feel empowered to be able to try out an idea.

- Culture of technology—teams realize that true innovation can be inspired by new technology and analysis of data, as well as by customers.

- Culture of business- and customer-savvy teams—teams, including developers, have a deep understanding of the business needs and constraints, and understanding of (and access to) the users and customers.

- Culture of skill-set and staff diversity—teams appreciate that different skills and backgrounds contribute to innovative solutions—especially engineering, design, and product.

- Culture of discovery techniques—the mechanisms are in place for ideas to be tested out quickly and safely (protecting brand, revenue, customers, and colleagues).

What does it really mean to have a strong execution culture?

- Culture of urgency—people feel like they are in wartime, and that if they don't find a way to move fast, then bad things could happen.

- Culture of high-integrity commitments—teams understand the need for (and power of) commitments, but they also insist on high-integrity commitments.

- Culture of empowerment—teams feel as though they have the tools, resources, and permission to do whatever is necessary to meet their commitments.

- Culture of accountability—people and teams feel a deep responsibility to meet their commitments. Accountability also implies consequences—not necessarily being terminated, except in extreme and repeated situations, but more likely consequences to their reputations among their peers.
- Culture of collaboration—while team autonomy and empowerment is important, teams understand their even higher need to work together to accomplish many of the biggest and most meaningful objectives.
- Culture of results—is the focus on output or is the focus on results?
- Culture of recognition—teams often take their cues from what is rewarded and what is accepted. Is it just the team that comes up with the great new idea that gets rewarded, or the team that delivered on a brutally tough commitment? And what is the message if missing a commitment is seen as easily excusable?

So, if these characteristics help define each culture, this begs some pretty tough questions:

- Is an innovation culture in any way inherently at odds with an execution culture?
- Does a strong execution culture lead to a stressful (or worse) work environment?
- What types of people, including leaders, are attracted to, and needed, for each type of culture?

I can tell you that there do exist companies that are very strong at both consistent innovation and execution. Amazon is one of the best examples. However, it's also well known that the Amazon work environment is not for the faint of heart. I've found that most companies that are exceptionally strong at execution are pretty tough places to work.

In my experience working with companies, only a few companies are strong at both innovation and execution. Many are good at execution but weak at innovation; some are strong at innovation and just okay at execution; and a depressing number of companies are poor at both innovation and execution (usually older companies that lost their product mojo a long time ago, but still have a strong brand and customer base to lean on).

In any case, what I hope you and your team will consider doing is assess yourself along these dimensions of innovation and execution, and then ask yourselves where you would like to be, or think you need to be, as a team or company.

Acknowledgments

The very nature of putting together this book on sharing best practices from the industry's best product companies means that I have learned from a great many exceptional people. I have been especially fortunate to have had the chance to work with and for some of our industry's best product minds and companies. I have learned from each one of these people, but some of them have made such a deep impression on me that I must thank them here.

First and foremost, my partners at the Silicon Valley Product Group. They are my colleagues now precisely because I have been so impressed with their talents and have learned so much from each of them over the years: Lea Hickman, Martina Lauchengco, and Chris Jones.

I must also thank Peter Economy, Jeff Patton, and Richard Narramore for their help reviewing and improving this book.

The genesis of this book was material developed at Netscape Communications. Netscape provided an unparalleled learning opportunity, and I gained much insight about product and leadership by working for and with truly brilliant minds, including Marc Andreessen, Barry Appelman, Jennifer Bailey, Jim Barksdale, Peter Currie, Eric Hahn, Basil Hashem, Mike Homer, Ben Horowitz, Omid Kordestani, Keng Lim, Bob Lisbonne, Debby Meredith, Mike McCue, Danny Shader, Sharmila Shahani, Ram Shriram, Bill Turpin, and David Weiden.

At eBay, I have to especially credit Marty Abbott, Mike Fisher, Chuck Geiger, Jeff Jordan, Josh Kopelman, Shri Mahesh, Pierre Omidyar, Lynn Reedy, Stephanie Tilenius, and Maynard Webb.

Each one of these people has directly influenced me and informed specific topics in this book, either by their explicit help and coaching or simply by way of their leadership and actions that I was fortunate enough to witness first hand.

While my time working for these exceptional companies was an invaluable learning experience, I found that as I began working with tech teams in my advisory and coaching work as part of SVPG, I benefited greatly by getting a chance to meet and work with the product leaders at many of the very best companies in our industry. There are simply too many people to list, but they know who they are, and I am grateful to every one of them.

This book is based on material produced for a blog and newsletter that I have published for many years, and each and every topic was improved thanks to feedback and comments from literally thousands of product managers and product leaders from every corner of the globe. I thank everyone who has read, shared, and commented on these articles.

Finally, those people who know the culture of the companies I've worked at understand that many very long hours were involved, and I could not have contributed to these companies without the support of my wife and children.

About the Author

Before founding the Silicon Valley Product Group to pursue his interests in helping others create successful products through his writing, speaking, advising, and coaching, Marty Cagan served as an executive responsible for defining and building products for some of the most successful companies in the world, including Hewlett-Packard, Netscape Communications, and eBay.

Marty began his career with a decade as a software engineer at Hewlett-Packard Laboratories, conducting research on software technology and building several software products for other software developers.

After HP, Marty joined a then-young Netscape Communications Corporation, where he had the opportunity to participate in the birth of the Internet industry. Marty worked directly for co-founder Marc Andreessen, where he was vice president for Netscape's platform and tools, and later e-commerce applications, and worked to help Internet startups and Fortune 500 companies alike understand and use the newly emerging technology.

Marty was most recently senior vice president of product and design for eBay, where he was responsible for defining products and services for the company's global e-commerce trading site.

During his career, Marty has personally performed and managed most of the roles of a modern software product organization, including engineering, product management, product marketing, user experience design, software testing, engineering management, and general management.

As part of his work with SVPG, Marty is an invited speaker at major conferences and top companies across the globe.

Marty is a graduate of the University of California at Santa Cruz with bachelor of arts degrees in computer science and applied economics (1981) and of the Stanford University Executive Institute (1994).

Learning More

The Silicon Valley Product Group website (www.svpg.com) is designed as a free and open resource where we share our latest thoughts and learnings from the world of technology-powered products.

You will also find examples of the techniques described in the book (see www.svpg.com/examples) as well as a current recommended reading list (see www.svpg.com/recommended-reading).

For aspiring product managers, we hold occasional intense training sessions, usually in San Francisco, New York City, and London. Our goal is to share the most recent learnings and to provide a career-defining experience for aspiring tech product managers (see www.svpg.com/public-workshops/).

For companies that believe they need dramatic and meaningful change across their technology and product organization to competitively produce technology-powered products, we also offer custom, on-site engagements.

You can find more information on these various options and learn more about the SVPG partners that provide these services, at www.svpg.com.

Index

Page references followed by *fig* indicate an illustrated figure.

A

A/B testing, 266

Adobe
consistent product innovation
by, 14
Creative Suite and Creative Cloud
of, 103–106
Lea Hickman of, 48, 103–106

AdWords (Google), 71–73

Agile at Scale, 295

Agile methods
as conducive to consistent
innovation, 295
inadequate application of, 20
leveraging the core principles
of, 24
product owner role in the, 50
in support of, 23–24
waterfall process versus, 17

Airbnb, 7

Amazon
consistent product innovation
by, 14
customer-centric culture
of, 315–316

customer letter technique
used by, 183–184, 185
product leadership of, 103

Analytics for quantitative value
testing, 267–270

Andreessen, Marc, 167

API platforms
customer discovery through, 202
developer misbehavior on public,
219

Apple
Camille Hearst of, 48, 307–308
consistent product innovation
by, 14
consumer device products by, 7
iTunes product, 307–308

Architecture
alignment of product team
with, 95–96
CTO responsibility to build
strong, 89
technical debt, 78, 319

Arnold, Kate, 48, 283–285

Audible, 7

Autonomy
   accountability tied to, 101–102
   company culture emphasis
      on leverage versus,
      100–101
   as principle of product team, 38
   product team structured for,
      94–95
   relationship between successful
      scaling and product
      team, 97–102

B
BBC
   Alex Pressland of the, 48,
      155–157
   "BBC Out of Home" product
      of, 156
Bezos, Jeff, 315–316
Blockbuster, 283, 285
Business accounting/finance skills,
   51–52
Business cases fatal flaw, 18
Business objectives
   CEO's responsibility for, 141
   for each product team,
      116–117
   OKR (objectives and key results)
      of products for, 137–138,
      139–141, 143–145,
      147–149
   See also Product Team objectives
Business results/outcomes
   execution culture with focus
      on, 325
   focusing on outputs instead of,
      108, 117
   leveraging technology for, 101

OKR (objectives and key results)
   of products, 137–138,
   139–141, 143–145,
   147–149
   outcome-based roadmaps, 118
   product manager's deep
      knowledge of your,
      44–45
Business strategy
   aligning product strategy
      with, 133
   focusing on outputs versus
      outcomes, 108, 117
Business viability risk, 165, 168
Business viability testing
   business development, 280
   challenges related to, 277–278
   customer success, 279
   description of, 173–174
   finance, 279–280
   legal, 280
   marketing, 278
   sales, 279
   security, 280

C
CEO of the Product, 277–278
Certified Scrum Product Owner
   class, 41
Chief Executive Officers (CEOs)
   being *CEO of the product*,
      277–278
   interest in business viability
      testing by, 281
   responsibility for organization's
      objectives and key
      results, 141

VP product position interview
    with, 83
who drives the product vision,
    81–82
Chief Information Officers
    (CIOs), 88
Chief Technology Officers (CTOs)
    comparing CIOs and, 88
    six major responsibilities of a,
        88–89
    leading the technology
        organization, 77, 87–88
    VP product position interview
        with, 83
    See also VP engineering
Collaboration
    company culture of, 325
    Lean and Agile principles, 24
    product team, 35
Communication
    of product learnings, 305–306
    of product strategy across the
        organization, 134
    story map as technique for,
        193–194
Company culture
    customer-centric, 315–316
    emphasis on autonomy versus
        leverage in, 100–101
    loss of velocity due to consensus,
        321
    See also Product culture
Computer programming skills, 51
Concierge testing technique,
    215–216
Consistent innovation
    Agile methods as conducive
        to, 295

challenge of maintaining, 13–14
definition of, 315
ideas leading to, 15–19, 55
top reasons for loss of, 315–317
Consumer device products, 7
Consumer products discovery
    program, 202–203
Consumer-service products, 7
Contextual inquiry, 212
Continuous discovery and delivery
    concept, 26–27*fig*
Corporate courage, 317
Creative Suite and Creative Cloud
    (Adobe), 103–106
Cue, Eddy, 308
Culture. *See* Company culture;
    Product culture
Customer-centric culture,
    315–316
Customer discovery program
    techniques
    applied to consumer products,
        202–203
    applied to customer-enabling
        tools, 202
    applied to platform/API products,
        202
    power of reference customers,
        196–198
    for qualitative value testing, 267
    recruiting the prospective
        reference customers, 199
    single target market, 198
    when to use the, 195–196
Customer-enabling tools, 202
Customer interviews
    different forms of the, 211–212
    return on your time, 213

Customer interviews (*Continued*)
  as important skill to have,
    211, 212
  tips on getting the most out of,
    212–213
Customer letter technique
  Amazon's applications
    of the, 183–184, 185
  description of the, 177
  Nordstrom's application of the,
    184–185
Customer misbehavior technique,
    217–218
Customer problems
  problems versus solutions,
    177–178
  opportunity assessment technique
    to identify the, 179, 180
Customers
  alignment of product team with
    users or, 96–97
  as always dissatisfied and wanting
    more, 316
  building relationship with
    prospective, 199–201
  concierge test technique used
    with, 215–216
  obsessing over competitors rather
    than your, 134
  opportunity assessment technique
    to identify target market,
    179, 180–181
  problem of too late product
    validation by, 20
  product evangelism by giving
    great demos to, 152
  product evangelism by sharing the
    pain of, 152

product manager's deep
    knowledge of the, 43–44
  reference, 196–198, 199
  unaware of what is possible with
    technology products, 166
Customer success strategy, 279

D
Data analysts, 68–69
Data knowledge, 44
Dedicated product teams, 33
Delivery managers
  description of and need for,
    91–92
  loss of velocity tied to lack of, 320
  Scrum Master role of, 91
  See also Product delivery
Demand testing techniques
  landing page demand test,
    254–255
  reasons for using, 253–254
Demos
  product evangelism by giving
    great, 152
  user test versus walkthrough
    versus product, 281–282
Design. *See* Product design
Design sprint technique, See
    Discovery Sprint
    technique.
Developer misbehavior
    technique, 219
Discovery coaches, 288, 289–290
Discovery framing techniques
  customer letter, 177, 183–185
  description of the, 171
  to ensure team is on the same
    page, 175

to identify all the big risks,
175–177
mistake to focus on solutions
instead of problems,
177–178
opportunity assessment, 177,
179–181
startup canvas, 177, 187–190
story map used for, 193–194
See also Risks
Discovery ideation techniques
concierge test, 215–216
customer interviews, 211–213
customer misbehavior, 217–218
description of the, 172
developer misbehavior, 219
hacks days, 221–222
story map used for, 193–194
when to use the, 208–209
See also Ideas
Discovery pivot, 130
Discovery planning techniques,
172, 191
customer discovery program,
195–203, 267
overview of the, 191
story map, 193–194
Discovery prototyping techniques
description of the, 172, 223
feasibility prototype, 229–231
hybrid prototype, 239–240
live-data prototype, 235–237
types of prototypes for,
224–225
user prototype, 233–234
See also Prototypes
Discovery Sprint technique,
287–289

Discovery testing techniques
overview of the, 172–173,
241–242
in risk-averse companies, 255–258
testing business viability, 173–174,
277–282
testing demand, 252, 253–255
testing feasibility, 173, 273–276
testing usability, 173, 243–249,
260–261
testing value, 173, 251–252,
259–262, 265–271
See also Risks
Doerr, John, 34
Durable product teams, 33

E
eBay
e-commerce of, 2
"Everything Else" category of, 218
Empowerment
accountability tied to, 101–102
company culture of, 324
innovation tied to product teams
with, 317
product team accountability
and, 34
Engineers
being brought in too late to
product development
process, 20
innovation tied to discovery
participation by, 316
loss of velocity tied to not
including them in
discovery, 320
making them feel like missionaries
not mercenaries, 61

Engineers (*Continued*)
  relationship between product
      managers and, 59–61
  tech lead role of, 61–62
  test automation, 69
Enterprise companies
  consistent product innovation
      challenge of, 13–14
Ethical risk, 168–169
Etsy, 7
Evangelizing
  by CTOs for technology
      organization, 89
  by product management, 151–153
  the product vision, 131
Execution product culture
  assessing your company's, 326
  characteristics of, 324–325
Experimentation culture, 324

F
Facebook
  consistent product innovation
      by, 14
  platform strategy of, 219
  product leadership of, 103
  as social media product, 7
Failed products
  Root Causes of Failed Product
      Efforts, 17–21
Feasibility prototypes, 224, 274
Feasibility prototype technique,
      229–231
Feasibility risk, 165, 166–168
Feasibility testing
  considering a feasibility prototype
      for, 224, 274
  description of, 173

  questions answered by, 273–274
  tips for successful, 274–275
Finances, 279–280
Fisher, Mike, 218
Founder product vision, 81–82
Front-end developers, 61

G
Gates, Bill, 206
Geiger, Chuck, 87
"Good Product Manager/Bad
      Product Manager"
      (Horowitz post), 312
Google
  consistent product innovation
      by, 14
  creation of the AdWords product
      of, 71–73
  Google Ventures (GV) team, 288
  Jane Manning of, 48, 71–73
  OKR (objectives and key results)
      approach used at, 137–138
  product leadership of, 103
Go to market (GTM), 127
Group product manager role
      (GPM), 83–85
Growth-stage companies
  how they devolve from good
      to bad, 301–304
  scaling to success challenges
      of, 11–12

H
Hack days
  two major benefits of, 222
  undirected vs. directed, 221
Hardware product discovery,
      275–276

Harik, Georges, 72
Hastings, Reed, 283
Hearst, Camille, 48, 307–308
Hewlett Packard (HP)
　management by objectives (MBO)
　　approach used at, 137
Hickman, Lea, 48, 103–106
High-fidelity user prototypes, 245
High-integrity commitments
　as alternative to product roadmap,
　　113, 115–120
　execution culture with, 324
　OKR (objectives and key results)
　　paired with, 140
　understanding how to get the best
　　results from, 118–120
Holistic view of product
　leadership roles in context
　　of, 77–78
　leaders of product design, 76–77
　leaders of product
　　management, 76
　leaders of technology
　　organization, 77
　understanding the concept
　　of, 25–26
Horowitz, Ben, 312
Hybrid prototypes, 225
Hybrid prototype technique,
　　239–240

I

Ideas
　as first step in product
　　development, 15–16*fig*
　problem with source of, 17–18
　understanding that most will
　　never work, 19

user testing to assess the value
　　of, 55
See also Discovery ideation
　　techniques; Innovation
Industrial design, 56
Industry knowledge, 45–46
Infrequent release cycles, 320
Innovation
　Agile methods as conducive
　　to consistent, 295
　challenge of maintaining
　　consistent product, 13–14
　definition of consistent, 315
　ideas leading to, 15–19, 55
　source of future, 100
　top reasons for loss of, 315–317
　See also Ideas; Scaling
Innovation product culture
　assessing your company's, 326
　characteristics of a, 323–324, 325
Instagram, 7
Interaction design, 56
Invite-only testing, 266–267
Iterations
　discovery, 287–289
　product discovery, 169–170
　the prototype, 262–263
　Sprint: (Knapp, Zeratsky, and
　　Kowitz) on, 288, 289
　time to money cost of
　　implementing, 19
IT-mindset organizations, 317
iTunes (Apple), 307–308

K

Kawasaki, Guy, 151
Keep The Lights On activities, 317
Knapp, Jake, 288

Knowing what we can't know
    lesson, 18
Kordestani, Omid, 72
Kowitz, Braden, 288

L
Landing page demand test, 254–255
Lauchengco, Martina, 48, 205–207
Leadership
    holistic view of, 75–78
    talent development role of, 75
    See also Product managers
Leadership roles
    product design, 76–77
    product management, 75
    technology organization, 77
    VP product, 79–85
Lean principles
    leveraging the core principles
        of, 24
    in support of, 23–24
Lean Startup coaches, 290
The Lean Startup (Ries), 29
Legal issues, 280
LinkedIn, 7
Live-data prototypes, 224
Live-data prototype technique,
    235–237
Lockhart, Walker, 184

M
Management By Objectives
    (MBO), 137
Manning, Jane, 48, 71–73
Markets
    focus on one target, 133
    go to market (GTM), 127

opportunity assessment technique
    to identify target, 179,
    180–181
    prioritizing, 126–127
    product manager's deep
        knowledge of your,
        45–46
    single target market technique
        for target, 198
    time to market (TTM), 127
    total addressable market (TAM),
        127
    See also Product/market fit
Mercenaries
    making engineers feel like
        missionaries and not, 61
    teams made of up, 34
Microsoft
    developing the Word for
        Mac of, 205–207
    Martina Lauchengco of, 48,
        205–207
Minimum Viable Product (MVP),
    29–30, 162, 287
Missionaries
    hack days used to build,
        221–222
    making engineers feel like, 61
    teams made up of, 34
Mission statements, 123

N
Netflix
    consistent product innovation
        by, 14
    consumer-service products of, 7
    Kate Arnold of, 48, 283–285
    product leadership of, 103

Netscape Communications,
    2, 72, 207
Nordstrom, 184–185

O

Objectives. *See* Business objectives;
    Product Team objectives
OKR (objectives and key results)
    critical points to remember when
        using, 139–141
    description and function of,
        137–138
    high-integrity commitments
        paired with, 140
    product team objectives approach
        using the, 143–145
    scaling the, 147–149
Opportunity assessment technique
    business objective, 179, 180
    customer problem, 179, 180
    description of the, 177
    key results question, 179, 180
    target market question, 179,
        180–181
Opportunity cost, 20–21
Outcome-based roadmaps, 118
Outcomes. *See* Business results
Output versus outcome, 108, 117

P

Packard, Dave, 137
Page, Larry, 71, 137
Patton, George, 137
Patton, Jeff, 193, 194
PayPal, 293
Pilot team technique, 291–292
Platform/API products, 202

Platform product teams, 148
The Power of Customer Misbehavior
    (Fisher), 218
Pressland, Alex, 48, 155–157
Priorities
    deciding on market, 126–127
    loss of velocity tied to rapidly
        shifting, 321
Product culture
    creating the right culture for
        success, 309
    description and importance of,
        82–83
    innovation versus execution,
        323–326
    VP product position who supports
        a strong, 83
    See also Company culture
Product delivery
    continuous discovery and,
        26–27*fig*
    CTO's responsibility for, 88
    understanding the purpose of, 28
    See also Delivery managers
Product demos
    product evangelism by giving
        great, 152
    user test versus walkthrough
        versus, 281–282
Product design
    the costs of absent, 56–58
    holistic user experience (UX),
        54–55
    industrial, 56
    interaction and visual, 56
    leaders of, 76–77
    loss of velocity tied to not utilizing
        in discovery, 320

Product design (*Continued*)
  user experience design team
      providing, 16–17
Product designers
  holistic user experience (UX)
      design by, 54–55
  interaction and visual
      design by, 56
  product discovery applied by,
      53–54
  prototyping by, 55
  user testing by, 55
Product development
  consistent product innovation
      requirement of, 13–14
  differences in the way best
      companies go about, 3
  growth-stage companies scaling to
      success with new, 11–12
  importance of integration to, 100
  importance of speed to, 99–100
  knowing what we can't know
      lesson on, 18
  problem in the role of, 19
  sources of future innovation, 100
  startups finding
      product/marketing fit,
      9–10
  waterfall process of, 15–21
  See also Engineering
Product development process
  Agile methods, 17, 20
  fatal flaws and root causes of
      failed, 17–21
  ideas starting the, 15–16*fig*, 17–18
  iterations ("sprints") 17, 19,
      169–170, 262–263,
      287–289

product deployed to customers, 17
  user experience design team
      providing designs, 16–17
  waterfall process, 15–21
Product discovery
  build things that don't scale
      philosophy of, 240
  continuous delivery and, 26–27*fig*
  critical risks addressed by, 165
  CTO's responsibility for, 89
  ethical risk examined through,
      168–169
  for hardware products, 275–276
  iterations of, 169–170
  loss of velocity tied to not
      including engineers in, 320
  loss of velocity tied to not utilizing
      design in, 320
  principles of addressing critical
      risks, 165–168
  product designer's application
      of, 53–54
  providing enough time for
      effective, 119
  validated product backlog
      output of, 27
  why it is so important, 161–163
Product discovery techniques
  customer discovery program,
      195–204, 267
  discovery framing, 171, 175–178,
      179–181, 183–185,
      187–190, 193–194
  discovery ideation, 172, 193–194,
      208–209, 211–213,
      215–216, 217–219,
      221–222
  discovery planning, 172, 191

discovery prototyping, 172,
223–225, 227–228,
229–231, 233–234,
235–237, 239–240
discovery sprint, 287–289
discovery testing, 172–173, 191,
241–242, 243–249,
251–263, 265–282
story map, 193–194
transformation, 174, 286
Product evangelism
of the product vision, 131
as "selling the dream," 151–153
Product foundational concepts
continuous discovery and delivery,
26–27*fig*
holistic product, 25–26
minimum viable product (MVP),
29–30, 162, 287
product delivery, 28
product discovery, 27
products and product/market
fit, 28
product vision, 29
prototypes, 27–28
See also specific foundational concept
Product learnings
communicating, 305–306
generous sharing of credit
and, 152
knowing what we can't know, 18
summarizing usability testing, 249
Product management
backlog administrator
model of, 41
leaders of, 76
management by objectives
(MBO), 137

OKR (objectives and key results),
137–138, 139–141,
143–145, 147–149
versus product owner role
responsibilities of, 42–46
roadmap administrator
model of, 41
why they want to have product
roadmaps, 109
Product manager responsibilities
deep knowledge of the customer,
43–44
deep knowledge of the data, 44
deep knowledge of your business,
44–45
deep knowledge of your market
and industry, 45–46
understanding the key, 42–43
Product managers
business accounting/finance
course recommended for,
51–52
computer programming
course recommended
for, 51
how they can work in order to be
successful, 41–42
innovation tied to strong, 316
loss of velocity tied to lack of
strong, 319
product owner versus the, 50
profiles and examples of the best,
48–50
relationship between engineers
and, 59–61
role and key responsibilities of,
5–6, 42–46
role in startups by, 9

Product managers (*Continued*)
   smart, creative, and persistent
      qualities of the best,
      46–48
   stakeholder management by,
      298–301
   VP product responsibility to
      develop strong team of,
      80–85
   See also Leadership
Product/market fit
   defining the, 203–204
   how consumer-focused companies
      structure the, 125
   importance of, 28
   sales organization's selling to
      markets with, 125–126
   Sean Ellis test for assessing,
      203–204
   startups finding their, 9–10
   See also Markets
Product marketing managers
   description of the, 63–64
   focus of the, 64–65
Product-mindset
      organizations, 317
Product objectives
   OKR (objectives and key results),
      137–138, 139–141,
      143–145
   using the OKR system at scale,
      147–149
   See also Business objectives
Product owner role, 50
Product principles, 135–136
Product roadmaps
   definition of, 108
   description and functions of, 18

high-integrity commitments as
      alternative to, 113,
      115–120, 140, 324
   outcome-based roadmaps, 118
   problems with, 19, 111–113
   stakeholder-driven roadmap form
      of, 108, 109
   two purposes of, 115–116
   typically focused on output not
      outcome, 108
   as typically the root cause of waste
      and failed efforts, 109
   weaning an organization off,
      293–294
   why management wants
      to have, 109
   why stakeholders are so attracted
      to, 294
Product strategy
   align business strategy with, 133
   applications of, 125–126
   business context provided by, 116
   description of the, 124
   innovation tied to focused, 316
   loss of velocity tied to lack of, 320
   principles of, 133–134
   product team structured to
      support, 95
   should be focused, 126
Product team principles
   development of techniques based
      on, 39–40
   team autonomy, 38
   team collaboration, 35
   team composition, 34
   team duration, 38
   team empowerment and
      accountability, 34

team location, 36
team of missionaries, 34
team reporting structure, 35
team scope, 36–37
team size, 35, 95
Product teams
  autonomy of, 38, 94–95, 97–102
  business objectives for each, 108,
    116–117
  challenges faced by growth-stage
    company, 11–12
  characteristics of good versus bad,
    311–314
  comprised of product manager
    and engineers, 6
  as cross-functional set of
    professionals, 143
  delivery manager's role in
    removing impediments
    for the, 91–92
  how to split up product across
    many, 94
  innovation tied to
    empowered, 317
  innovation tied to stable, 316
  loss of velocity tied to lack
    of co-located and
    durable, 320
  OKR (objectives and key results)
    applications by, 143–145
  OKR (objectives and key results)
    scaling by, 147–149
  principles of strong, 33–40
  principles of structuring,
    93–102
  share learnings and credit
    generously, 152
  three team skill levels of, 99

understand that *It's all about
    the product team*, 32
Product vision
  business context provided by, 116
  CEO or founder type of, 81–82
  description and purpose of, 29, 81,
    123–124
  innovation tied to compelling, 316
  loss of velocity tied to lack of, 320
  principles of, 129–131
  product evangelism by sharing
    the, 152
  product team structured to
    support, 95
  should be inspiring, 126, 130
  when there is no clear visionary
    driving, 81
Profiles
  Alex Pressland, 48, 155–157
  Camille Hearst, 48, 307–308
  Jane Manning, 48, 71–73
  Lea Hickman, 48, 103–106
  Martina Lauchengco, 48, 205–207
  Kate Arnold
Programmers. *See* Engineers
Programming skills, 51
Prototypes
  description and function of, 27–28
  feasibility, 224, 274
  high-fidelity user, 245
  hybrid, 225
  iterating the, 262–263
  live-data, 228
  minimum viable product (MVP),
    29–30, 162, 287
  principles of, 227–228
  product designer's prototyping
    of, 55

Prototypes (*Continued*)
  product evangelism by using, 152
  testing your, 246–248
  user, 224, 233–234
  user test versus product demo
        versus walkthrough for
        showing, 281–282
  visiontype, 123
  Wizard of Oz, 240
  See also Discovery prototyping
        techniques
Public APIs, 219

Q
QA testing, 17
Qualitative value testing
  begin with an interview, 260
  description of, 252, 259–260
  specific value tests, 261–262
  usability test, 260–261
Quantitative value testing
  A/B testing, 266
  customer discovery program, 267
  description of, 252, 265–266
  flying blind when, 271–272
  invite-only testing, 266–267
  role of analytics in, 267–270

R
Recognition culture, 325
Reference customers
  recruiting the prospective, 199
  understanding the power of,
        196–198
Ries, Eric, 29
Risks
  addressed by product
        discovery, 165

business viability, 165, 168
  ethical, 168–169
  feasibility, 165, 166–168
  usability, 165, 167
  value, 165, 166
Roadmap administrator model, 41
Robinson, Frank, 29

S
Sales-driven specials model,
        17–18
Salesforce.com, 7
Sales organizations
  aligning product strategy to
        strategy of the, 134
  Google AdWords opposed by
        Google's, 72
  selling to markets with
        product/market fit,
        125–126
  testing business viability benefits
        to, 279
Scaling
  Agile at Scale consultancies
        on, 295
  build things that don't scale
        philosophy of product
        discovery, 240
  as growth-stage company
        challenge, 11–12
  keep the lights on activities, 317
  the OKR system, 147–149
  product team autonomy to
        facilitate, 97–102
  structuring product teams
        for effective, 93–102
  understanding that the right talent
        drive, 74

See also Innovation; Products; Technology-powered products

Scrum Master role, 91

Sean Ellis test, 203–204

Security issues, 280

Shared services product teams, 148

Silicon Valley Product Group, 106, 207

Single target market technique, 198

Skill-set diversity culture, 324

Social media products, examples of, 7

Sonos, 7

Source of ideas problem, 17–18

Sprint: How to Solve Big Problems and Test New Ideas in Just Five Days (Knapp, Zeratsky, and Kowitz), 288, 289

Sprints. *See* Iterations
  in discovery See Discovery Sprints
  in delivery, See Scrum Sprints

Stakeholder management
  product manager responsibilities for, 298–299
  strategies for successful, 299–301

Stakeholders
  defining, 297–298
  interest in business viability testing by, 281
  product evangelism by giving great demos to key, 152
  stakeholder-driven products using ideas from, 17–18
  stakeholder-driven roadmap, 108, 109
  why they are so attracted to roadmaps, 294

Startup canvas technique
  description of the, 177
  tackling the biggest risks first using the, 188–190
  when to use the, 187–188

Startups
  discovery testing in, 255–257
  finding their product/marketing fit, 9–10
  founders driving product vision in, 81–82

Story map technique, 193–194

T

Target markets
  opportunity assessment technique to identify, 179, 180–181
  single target market technique for, 198

Technical debt, 78, 319

Technology
  company culture of, 324
  maturity of, 101

Technology organizations
  CTO's six responsibilities to the, 88–90
  leadership of the, 77, 87–90

Technology-powered products
  consistent product innovation challenge of, 13–14
  customers as always wanting more and better, 316
  description and examples of, 7–8
  discovery for hardware products, 275–276
  Google AdWord, 71–73
  growth-stage companies scaling to success with, 11–12

Technology-powered products (*Continued*)
  root causes of failed, 15–21
  startups finding product/marketing fit, 9–10
  See also Products; Scaling
Tesla, 7
Test automation engineers, 69
Time to market (TTM), 127
Time to money, 112
Total addressable market (TAM), 127
Transformation techniques, 174, 286
Twitter, 7

U
Uber, 7
University of California, Berkeley, 207
Urgency culture, 324
Usability risk, 165, 167
Usability testing
  description of, 173, 243–244
  preparing the test, 245–246
  qualitative, 260–261
  recruiting users to test, 244–245
  summarizing the learning from the, 249
  testing your prototype, 246–248
User experience design teams, 16–17
User experience (UX) design, 54–55
User prototypes, 224, 233–234
User researchers, 68

User Story Mapping: Discover the Whole Story, Build the Right Product (Patton), 194
User testing
  description of, 55
  product demo versus walkthrough versus, 281–282

V
Validated product backlog, 27
Value risk, 165, 167
Value testing
  description of, 173, 251–252
  qualitatively, 252, 259–262
  quantitatively, 252, 265–271
  testing demand, 252
Value tests
  using access to demonstrate value, 262
  using money to demonstrate value, 261
  using reputation to demonstrate value, 261–262
  using time to demonstrate value, 262
Vision pivot, 130
Vision. *See* Product vision
Visiontype, 123
Visual design, 56
VP engineering, 77
  See also Chief technology officers (CTOs)
VP product
  competencies required for the, 80–83
  description and titles of the, 79
  group product manager (GPM) type of, 83–85

W
Walkthrough, 282
Waterfall process
    Agile methods versus, 17
    product development fatal flaws
        of the, 17–21
    product development using the,
        15–17
Wizard of Oz prototype,
    240

Word for Mac (Microsoft), 205–207
Workday, 7
Workiva, 7

Y
YouTube, 73, 308

Z
Zeratsky, John, 288